JOEL NEDERH

THE FOREVER PEOPLE

LIVING TODAY IN THE LIGHT OF ETERNITY

CRC Publications
Grand Rapids, Michigan

P&R Publishing
Phillipsburg, New Jersey

The Forever People: Living Today in the Light of Eternity. Copublished by CRC Publications, 2850 Kalamazoo Ave. SE, Grand Rapids, MI 49560; and P&R Publishing, P.O. Box 817, Phillipsburg, NJ 08865.

We welcome your comments. Call us at 1-800-3000 or e-mail us at editors@crcpublications.org.

Library of Congress Cataloging-in-Publication Data
Nederhood, Joel H.
    The forever people: living today in the light of eternity / Joel Nederhood.
      p. cm.
    ISBN 1-56212-542-7
    1. Christian life—Meditations. 2. Future life—Christianity—Meditations.
  3. Christian life—Christian Reformed authors. I. Title.
    BV4501.2.N393 2000
    248.4—dc21

                                        00-046835

10 9 8 7 6 5 4 3 2 1

CONTENTS

Preface. 6
 1 Eternity Within 8
 2 Forever People 10
 3 Eternal Life 12
 4 Children of Our Heavenly Father 14
 5 Our Dwelling Place 16
 6 Between Two Trees. 18
 7 The Covenant Connection 20
 8 Covenant Breakers 22
 9 Faith and Walking 24
10 Father Abraham. 26
11 Faith = Obedience 28
12 Driven by Faith 30
13 Who Goes to Heaven? 32
14 Wendy's Family 34
15 The Inheritance We Share 36
16 Behind Closed Doors. 38
17 Our Father? 40
18 A Word of Caution 42
19 How We Hallow 44
20 Remember Me. 46
21 Hitting Delete 48
22 The Bread of Heaven 50
23 No, Not Again! 52
24 Our Cry for Help 54
25 Praying in the Spirit. 56
26 Wanting His Wants 58
27 Praying for Each Other 60
28 The Forever Sign 62
29 Remaining in Christ. 64
30 The Mystical Union. 66
31 How to Live Forever 68
32 Win/Win. 70
33 Orphans Not. 72
34 Keeping in God's Love 74
35 Living in the Temple 76
36 Overcoming Our Brokenness 78
37 The Church of the Firstborn 80

38 The Un-cozy Church 82
39 Longing for Communion 84
40 Sustained by His Body 86
41 Samuel's Grandson 88
42 Jumpin' Jehoshaphat 90
43 When Forever Began 92
44 See the Rainbow 94
45 The James Factor 96
46 Recognizing Jesus 98
47 How Many Angels? 100
48 Living by Faith 102
49 Craps 104
50 Meaningful Meaningless Lives 106
51 T4G = T4H 108
52 The Circle 110
53 Hating This Life 112
54 Our Own Worst Enemy 114
55 Our Lust, Our Pride 116
56 Affluenza 118
57 Laying Up Treasure 120
58 Acting Like a Kid 122
59 The Grand Cherokee 124
60 Ko Pha-Ngan 126
61 Instead of Futility 128
62 "Holy, Holy, Holy!" 130
63 The Meaning of Love 132
64 Why We Blow It 134
65 Reading Ezekiel 136
66 Listening Helps 138
67 Heaven Is Not Just for Music Majors 140
68 Oddballs 142
69 Think Pure 144
70 Experiencing Christ's Resurrection 146
71 First Things 148
72 Schizoid Christians 150
73 Wretched Travelers 152
74 "Stinkin' Thinkin'" 154
75 The Alibi Agency 156

76 What Joseph Saw 158
77 Eternal Fathers 160
78 Husband Love 162
79 Hosea Love 164
80 The Forgiving Mode 166
81 The Note of Joy 168
82 When the Rubber Hits the Road 170
83 Pleasing the Spirit 172
84 Gentlemen 174
85 My Amaryllis 176
86 Counterfeit Miracles 178
87 The Battle of the Red Dragon 180
88 Swallowing Herring 182
89 The Glory Road 184
90 Meanwhile, Back on Planet Earth 186
91 Pleasure Seekers, Pleasure Finders 188
92 How We Know 190
93 Airborne 192
94 Will I Know Stephanie? 194
95 The Schedule 196
96 God Will Not Forget 198
97 The Heavenly Printout 200
98 Pella Justice 202
99 Finishing Strong 204
100 The Deeds That Follow 206

Preface

Let me be honest. At first I did not want to write this book this way. I wanted to write it as a "book" book—not as a book of meditations.

As I read the Bible over the years, I became more and more overwhelmed with the inescapable conclusion that we human beings are much greater than we ordinarily tend to think of ourselves. Sometimes we are very proud; at other times, we can be crushed with feelings of inadequacy. But seldom are we lifted by the realization that, whatever our emotions at any given moment, we are actually much like God, and we are destined to live as his imagebearers forever.

I began to write about this glory in a book with chapters. Gradually, I realized that such a book about our eternal destiny wouldn't help because it would tend to turn our *forever* into a subject among other subjects. Few readers would take the time to follow the argument and consult the biblical material. Where the pages that I first wrote are, I do not know. I have mislaid them. Thankfully.

So I have turned to the meditation mode. It is better to *savor* our eternity, to let the sentences the Spirit wrote appear first, and then to think about their meaning and their implications. So some of what follows is actually about our eternity; it dwells on what has been revealed about the grandeur of our future. But much of it is actually mundane—it is about the implications of our eternity for our day-to-day lives. Those who know they are going to live forever will live differently from those who believe they are temporary critters.

A book with chapters and such would give the impression that our *foreverness* is something we can grasp. But we cannot. So we look at the sentences that make sense only if we are going to live with God forever, and let them possess us. We are not learning about a subject that lies still while we examine it; it lies beyond our stretched-out minds. It taunts our earthbound wits, bogged down as they are in conventional wisdom that is like earth dust, not like the galaxies.

Genome, DNA, and all that aside, we have eternity as a component from the moment of conception. It is our eternity that defines us. Every human being has an eternal destiny, and every decision and every action has eternal consequences. If a person rejects Christ Jesus during this earthly adventure, the eternal consequences are too horrible to contemplate. If, by Christ's grace, we "receive the Savior," as John 1:18 puts it, the glory that will surely come will cause us to forget our time-bound suffering the way a mother forgets her birth agony when her newborn is laid upon her breast.

These are subjects we talk about when someone dies, in hushed tones at funeral homes. They are subjects we expect clergy to touch on often enough to assuage our grief and kindle our courage. But we have not learned always to think of ourselves as people whose every thought and action has its forever consequences. Our eternity should have consequences for today because we know that today is part of something grand and lasting. We are always to be thinking of the next phase of our existence, the glory phase. Just as a miserable GI fantasizes about his discharge and return to his beloved, Christ-believers are encouraged by the remembrance of their future.

So here is a book of meditations about our *foreverness*. And is this better than a book with chapters? To some degree. But is it really helpful? I pray so. Yet, when we think of our small selves and of the marvelous future we are promised, what a crumpled inadequacy these pages are! The greatness of God cannot be caught by our vocabulary, nor by our puny minds. To say with fervor that God is great is a trembling whisper within the unfathomable universe; it is a sublime sentiment from our point of view, but compared to the infinity of God's power and his glory, it is a nothing. But this great God is love itself, and he has done all that is necessary to insure that all who love the Son, Christ Jesus, will enjoy membership in his household, now and forever. We shall sit at God's table, children of our heavenly Father.

If this life is exciting, just think what forever is going to be!

Joel Nederhood
August 2000

ONE

Eternity Within

[God] has . . . set eternity in the hearts of men. . . .
—Ecclesiastes 3:11

Have you ever thought it strange that we find it hard to accept our fate? Few willingly acquiesce when they learn that their adventure here on earth is doomed from the start.

When my sister wrote about her decades-long battle with cancer, she told how it felt to embrace her husband after she was finally told there was no longer any hope for a cure. She felt herself leaving while he was still firmly rooted in this life. That her time of embracing would likely come to an end while he would remain here crushed her and made her call out in anguish.

Why are we like this? Why can we not simply receive news like this and get on with our lives as long as we can? The answer is in the enigmatic book of Ecclesiastes, which tells us simply that we cannot accept such reality because we are not creatures who were meant to die. We are too much like God for that.

We learn in this third chapter that God has set eternity in our hearts. Ah, yes, this could be the reason we love life so much, why we cling to it with such tenacity and are crushed when we can no longer put off confronting our death.

We must be careful when we deal with poetic material like this—we might be tempted to set it aside as just so much sentiment. But this is the Bible, after all, and the statement is straightforward. There is actually much here that can help us understand ourselves better, much that can teach us why we do not want to accept our plight, and also much that can give us hope.

The Teacher uses a slippery word for *eternity* here that tantalizes us as we seek to grasp its meaning. The beloved King James Version translates the sentence by saying that God has set the *world* in our hearts; this signifies that within each person is a tie to all the universe. Frequently the word is translated *forevermore,* as in Psalm 133:3, which announces that in Mount Zion, the Lord "bestows his blessing, even life forevermore."

God has placed *forevermore* in our hearts. We are born with attachments to forever. Though our own existence begins at the time of our conception, the fact that God is the one who creates us connects us with God's eternity; once we are created by the eternal God, we are involved in forever.

God has placed eternity in our hearts. Isn't this likely the reason we have these undeniable feelings that we should go on forever? God has placed this desire in our *hearts* after all; we are not talking about something that might be merely psychological. In the Bible the heart is the controlling element of each person's life. Human beings are impressed with externals—clothing, make-up, hair, youth—but God looks within and announces that what is in our hearts is what is important about us. Jesus said that the pure in heart would see God. The heart is the controlling element of every life.

And isn't it true that we actually do feel as if we are eternal? When we look inside, we find feelings, longings, and aspirations that can be explained only by the fact that something about each of us transcends what we are by nature. It cannot be explained by our chemical makeup nor by neurology. It can be explained only by the fact that we have this close contact with God, who made us and who put eternity within us. So even though there is external evidence that we are not going to be around forever, we know that our future extends far beyond what is ordinarily considered its termination. It is impossible for us to be terminally ill.

We should think about eternity more than we do; in fact, we should think about it all the time. When we experience those blessed attachments to other people—spouses, children, parents, nieces and nephews, friends—and when we shudder and begin to weep because we know we are going to have to leave each other, we should view these very feelings as evidence that we are more than finite creatures.

It is a glorious thing to be a human being. Once God creates us, we are going to last forever. That knowledge should fill us with excitement every moment, every day. Much of our discomfort and sense of longing is caused by our ardent desire to be so much more than we can be. And we feel this way because of eternity within us.

Eternal God, make me sensitive in this day to the eternity you
have created within me. Let this be my hope and joy today. Amen.

TWO

Forever People

"Whoever lives and believes in me will never die."
—John 11:26

N ever say never. We have all said that to ourselves; we have all had others say it to us. Good advice. Most of us have found ourselves doing something we never thought we would, possibly something so good it was mind-boggling, and we have been overcome with joy. But if ten years ago we had said this would *never* happen, along with our joy might come embarrassment.

Once I was taking care of a young boy, about four years old, when the dentist called and reminded me that I was forgetting my appointment. I hurried to his office, taking the little guy with me. As I sat in the chair, with the dentist inserting his whining drill into my gaping maw, my young and terrified companion, sitting cross-legged in the corner, solemnly declared: "I don't never want to go to the dentist forever."

Jesus said something like that about those who believe in him: such people will absolutely not die forever. He said "never" with all the power language can muster. Jesus' friend Martha must not have been able to hide her puzzlement. After making his statement, Jesus asked her point-blank: "Do you believe this, or don't you?"

Do believers believe this? That is the question. Of course they believe lots of things. They can say the Apostles' Creed in thirty-three seconds, but sometimes the amen at the end is like a fastener that snaps shut. Then they put the creed away until next Sunday. The creed concludes on the same note Jesus struck in his conversation with Martha: "I believe in the resurrection of the body and the life everlasting." But you see, we say that creed in church. We believe it, yes, we do—in church, but not out at the cemetery where winter winds blow fierce as we stand by an open grave.

Jesus did not make this statement in a church on Sunday. He made it on the way to the tomb where the body of his good friend Lazarus was decomposing. No embalmer's art had preserved him for four days so that Jesus could see him after his journey from the land east of the Jordan. Mary and Martha had put him away quickly, as the custom was, and they had joined the mourners in their weeping. It was one of those dark and dismal times that descends on us when death pushes everything else aside and demands our undivided attention.

Jesus knew all this. But he knew so much more. He was not only on his way to a repulsive tomb, but he was on his way to his own tomb; within days, he would occupy the same place Lazarus then occupied. But there would be none of death's stench when he was laid to rest; his glory would transform that cramped and dreadful place. In that place the Holy Spirit of the living God would come and touch his wounded, mutilated corpse, and life would flow through it like a mighty elixir. He would rise majestically, carefully folding the headpiece of the dead he had been wearing.

So he said to Martha, "I am the resurrection and the life." Throughout his ministry, Jesus had issued solemn statements with the words "I am." "I am this" and "I am that" and "I am something else." Each statement helps us understand Jesus, but none gives us more hope than this one: "I am the resurrection." This message is repeatedly attached to Christ: *he is life.* "In him was life, and that life was the light of men" (John 1:4). And here in John 11 we find the ultimate revelation: If you believe in Jesus, his life becomes your possession.

What follows from all this is that if you believe in Jesus, you cannot die. How can you? Faith unites us to Christ. When we have faith we are *in* Christ. How can a person who is in Christ die? It is impossible.

I imagine that Jesus would like to take us by our shoulders on those days when our chins are on our chests and we are so sad because we see the end of the road for ourselves or for someone we love. He would like to take us by the shoulders and shake some sense into us.

How can we go on living, terrified by death as we are? We shall not die if we believe in Christ. He is not playing games with us; he is telling us the truth. This is no figure of speech. It will look like death, of course it will, but looks have nothing to do with it. Christ has everything to do with it. Faith has everything to do with it.

Living Christ, help me to believe this, really believe. Let my understanding that I am forever affect what I do this day, what I say, and how much I smile. Amen.

THREE

Eternal Life

"This is eternal life: that they may know you, the only true God, and Jesus Christ, whom you have sent."
—John 17:3

E ternal life stretches backward and forward. We tend to think of eternal life as something in the future, hopefully in the distant future (if we're frank about it). At best we think of it as a vacation we are going to take way, way down the road. It will be fine when we get there, but let's not get too excited about it now.

When we listen in to Jesus praying to his heavenly Father just before going to the cross, we discover that eternal life starts in the present. In fact, what he says tells us that eternal life is not so much a life that stretches along an eternal time line on and on forever ahead of us; actually, it doesn't have very much, if anything, to do with time at all. It is a state, a condition, a relationship with the only true God.

Jesus' prayer in John 17 is often called the high priestly prayer. That it is included in the sacred record is a dramatic expression of the Holy Spirit's inspiration of the Bible. Jesus had promised that he would send the church the Holy Spirit, whom he called "the Counselor." "The Holy Spirit, whom the Father will send in my name, will teach you all things and will remind you of everything I have said to you" (John 14:26). John wrote this gospel about fifty years after Jesus prayed this prayer, and the Holy Spirit enabled him to write it.

So, as Jesus prays, we are allowed to eavesdrop. The prayer begins with a comment that reminds us of the mystery of salvation itself, as Jesus talks with his Father in heaven about his mission. What was his mission? To do whatever was necessary to give eternal life to all those his Father had given him. Jesus' mission was designed to accomplish a very specific goal. It was not as if he came here, taught and died and rose again, and then waited around to see who would take an interest in what he had done. Not at all. There was a specific group of people whom the Father knew and whom he had given to his Son. All of Jesus' power and authority had been given him so that he could accomplish his mission to provide these people—and only these people—with eternal life.

We also find a reference to Jesus' Father and these people in John 10. Here Jesus is very outspoken about the fact that only those whom the Father has given to him will be able to respond to his message. Others will hear it, but it will sail right over their heads. "My sheep listen to my voice; I know them and they follow me. I give them eternal life, and they shall never perish; no one can snatch them out of my hand. My Father, who has given them to me, is greater than all; no one can snatch them out of my Father's hand. I and the Father are one" (John 10:27-30).

In John 10 and 17, Jesus talks about giving eternal life to this special group of people whom Jesus' Father knows. We learn that these people also know the Father . . . and the Son. Eternal life has something to do with knowledge—first of all the knowledge the Father has of his children, and second the knowledge the children have of their Father and of Christ Jesus.

We have eternal life when we know the only true God and the one whom the only true God has sent into this world, Jesus Christ. God knows his people, and they know God. Once that knowledge relationship is in place, God's people have eternal life. *Know*, in this case, means more than collecting information off God's web page. The best illustration of this knowledge is the knowledge a husband and wife have of each other in a good marriage. The Bible actually uses the word *know* for coitus in some places, but the knowledge a husband and wife have of each other goes far beyond that. A husband and wife who love each other and who have lived together for many years have a deep and tender relationship that is characterized by intimate knowledge of one another. They keep nothing back from each other. They talk about the most sensitive subjects. They know each other so well that they are virtually one. Believers are able to know God and his Son Jesus in a way that is something like this, and this is the way God the Father knows them.

Eternal life begins right now. Today. In this moment. Forever people know the reality of such a life.

Your grace, O God, is immeasurable. We are overwhelmed by your knowledge of us; now help us learn to know you better. We want to experience eternal life already in our humble lives. For Jesus' sake, Amen.

FOUR

Children of Our Heavenly Father

Jesus knew . . . that he had come from God and was returning to God.
—John 13:3

A s Jesus was about to perform one of the most dramatic acts of his earthly ministry—washing his disciples' feet—this sublime thought filled his mind: I have come from God, and I am on my way back to God.

Can you and I think this way about ourselves? May we begin our day by saying, "I have come from God, and I am on my way back to God?"

The astounding answer to that question is yes. When Jesus taught his disciples to pray, he told them that they should address God by saying, "Our Father in heaven . . . " When he did that he was actually inviting us to think of ourselves as people who have come from God and are returning to God.

Now, we have not come from God in the same way Jesus did. But we have come from God. We are not the product of a chance mixing of genes; we are God's workmanship. And not only has God controlled what happened when we were "woven together in the depths of the earth" (Ps. 139:15), but the Bible supports the idea that God knew those who would believe in Christ before their birth.

Ephesians 1:4 tells us that believers in Christ were chosen in him "before the creation of the world. . . . " Romans 8:29 speaks about those whom God "foreknew"—they are the people who believe and are ultimately glorified. In other words, even before our conception, God knows us by name; once we exist in God's mind, he arranges our lives to insure that we will be born at precisely the time we should be born, with exactly the characteristics we should have. God controls every experience of our lives as he prepares us for eternity in his presence.

So when Jesus says we should call God "our Father in heaven," he is not using a figure of speech; he is speaking of reality. Our real Father is in heaven, just as Jesus' real Father was in heaven. "To those who believed in his name, he gave the right to become children of God—children born not of natural descent, nor of human decision or a husband's will, but born of God" (John 1:12-13).

We always think of our human father as primary, and when we talk about our heavenly Father, we are using a figure of speech. We tend to say to ourselves, Of course, my real father is Arthur (or whatever his name happens to be). But that's not true. Our real Father is God—we have come from God. God uses our human fathers to accomplish his will.

We should remember that Jesus had an earthly father too, and while he was in this world, his earthly father established Jesus' identity. "'Is this not Jesus, the son of Joseph, whose father and mother we know?'" (John 6:42). Joseph, who was of David's line, established Jesus of Nazareth as the Son of David. Joseph was Jesus' adoptive father, and Mary took him very seriously. Once when she was upset with Jesus, she reprimanded him: "Son, why have you treated us like this? Your father and I have been anxiously searching for you" (Luke 2:48). Mary did not believe in the virgin birth of Christ as we must; she experienced it. But she called Joseph Jesus' father. Yes, Jesus had an earthly father, but he always knew that he had come from God and was returning to God. Like Jesus, we have an earthly father, but we have come from God and are returning to God.

So when Jesus met Mary Magdalene after his resurrection, he told her to go to the disciples and tell them, "'I am returning to my Father and your Father, to my God and your God'" (John 20:17).

Teach us to pray, Lord—we go to Jesus with this request. And he tells us that he will, but he wants us to remember, right from the get-go, whom we are praying to. Prayer is not a psychological state that will help people get over pneumonia or depression. It is communication with the only true God, who is our heavenly Father. When we talk to God, our cell phones are connected to another realm, the realm where our Father is, the realm where he conceived of us in his mind.

At this time, we are earthly creatures. But through faith in Christ, we are actually heavenly creatures. We have come from God, and we are returning to God. That's what Jesus did. When we believe in him, we are clothed with Christ, and our heavenly Father always deals with us as his own children.

Our Father in heaven, receive us in this moment as your children.
Calm our troubled spirits, inspire us with the joyful knowledge
that we have come from you, and energize us with your Spirit
as we continue our journey home. In Christ, Amen.

FIVE

Our Dwelling Place

Lord, You have been our dwelling place throughout all generations.
—Psalm 90:1

I t is intriguing to try to figure out what Moses has in mind here. He has God's eternity in view: "from everlasting to everlasting you are God" (v. 2). The everlasting God is where we live. The trouble with trying to understand this is that we know so little about God. But there's another problem too: we don't know very much about dwelling places either.

Listen to the people talking in the Business Center, Red Carpet Club, O'Hare Airport: "Hi, Hon. . . . Just wanted you to know that the flight to Narita is delayed; so won't be able to meet Shojiru when I get there. And I will probably miss my flight to Hong Kong. I'll e-mail you as soon as I can. Love you. . . . "

What do people who gallop through life know about dwelling places? They're seldom home for very long. Or they have two or three houses, places where they hang their hats—one they live in during the summer and the other when the snow is piling up in Minneapolis.

A dwelling place is the environment that defines a person. We have to have a dwelling place if we are going to find out who we really are. We can't understand ourselves if we ricochet through life virtually homeless.

God has a dwelling place, apparently. What must this be? We can only conclude that God's dwelling place is himself. Where else could God dwell—what other place would be big enough to be his dwelling? In the Old Testament, God said he would put his name within the temple Solomon built and added, "My eyes and my heart will always be there" (1 Kings 9:3). Yes, that's true, but it's also true, as Solomon said in the prayer he used to dedicate the temple, "The heavens, even the highest heaven, cannot contain you" (1 Kings 8:27). Ultimately God's dwelling place is God.

Moses came as close to this dwelling place as anyone. "The LORD would speak to Moses face to face, as a man speaks with his friend" (Ex. 33:11). The five books of Moses close with these words: "No prophet has risen in Israel like Moses, whom the LORD knew face to face . . ." (Deut. 34:10).

What did Moses have in mind when he said that the Lord has always been *our* dwelling place? Surely this exalted statesman didn't have ordinary people in mind when he wrote this, did he? What's astonishing about Psalm 90 is that Moses *is* writing about you and me and himself as garden-variety men and women who do pretty well until we are seventy, and then our bodies start to fall apart. It's astonishing that he writes this way, considering that his own life span was 120 years, and when he died he still walked like he did when he was a shepherd and he could still read the *Desert Times* without glasses. He describes us with uncanny accuracy: seventy years, okay; eighty, maybe; ninety, well, you are going to have problems if you didn't have them earlier.

Psalm 90 is about individual men and women, uneasy that they may have accomplished little, turning over their lives and asking the everlasting Lord to make something of them. The psalm calls us to wake up and be sensible about where we are along life's time line: "Teach us to number our days aright, that we may gain a heart of wisdom" (v. 12).

There's a lot of gloom in Psalm 90, references to God's wrath and to us as grass that the sun withers, but the overall impact is one of uplifting victory. Here is a call for gladness just when affliction crumples our fragile feelings: "Satisfy us in the morning with your unfailing love, that we may sing for joy and be glad all our days" (v. 14). Please Lord, show us and our children your splendor.

There is no place in the world big enough for God to dwell in but himself. And there is no place big enough for us except God. God surrounds us with his power and love. God assures us that he has known us before the first mountain thrust skyward, and he will know us forever.

Today, those who trust in Jesus Christ, God's ultimate revelation, remember Moses, who on at least two occasions spent forty uninterrupted days in God's dwelling place, whose face was dazzling after he had spent time with him, and they take him at his word. God is our dwelling place.

Help me to remember that you will forever be my dwelling place. You are as near to me and I to you as I am near to my own heart. Make me glad today, O Lord, even if afflictions come. In Jesus' name, Amen.

SIX

Between Two Trees

"I will give him the right to eat from the tree of life,
which is in the paradise of God."
—Revelation 2:7

According to the Bible, the history of our race is being played out between two trees: the tree of life in the original paradise and the tree of life in the paradise of God.

Genesis 2 describes the situation in the earthly paradise. At its center stood two trees, one a mortal threat, the other alive with life eternal. "And the Lord God made all kinds of trees grow out of the ground—trees that were pleasing to the eye and good for food. In the middle of the garden were the tree of life and the tree of the knowledge of good and evil" (v. 9).

Our curiosity is piqued as we think of those two trees growing side by side, so different from each other. Like the other trees in the garden, these were beautiful, each day enticing our first parents with tantalizing fruit. As our parents roamed the garden they could eat as they pleased; only the fruit of one tree was forbidden.

The fruit of the tree of life was not forbidden. Did they eat it, then, along with all the rest? Was it the food of this tree that gave them their unending energy? Or did they never touch its fruit? Would they be granted the right to eat of it after they had passed their test?

We have no answer to these questions. All we know is that the tree of life was there and that the Bible records no restrictions regarding eating its fruit. Whatever the situation, we do know that once they had eaten the forbidden fruit, a new danger existed within paradise: if they ate the fruit of the tree of life, these poor sinners would live forever in their sin.

Genesis 3 records a divine conversation that tells us that our first parents were banished from the garden of their innocence so that they would not eat of the fruit of the life-giving tree. "The man has now become like one of us, knowing good and evil. He must not be allowed to reach out his hand and take also from the tree of life and eat, and live forever" (v. 22). So they were sent out, with a flaming cherubim sword flashing on the path that led to the tree of life. Our poor, poor race was doomed from that day on to live out its days east of Eden.

How should we understand all this? This is a history before ordinary history, and along with reality it contains deep symbolism. What eventually happened to the tree of life? Did it eventually just die, one of a kind, never to appear again? In fact, what happened to the garden itself? Over time, as sinful degradation infected all nature, was it all simply assimilated into the rest of creation?

Now there is nothing that can withstand the advance of death in this damned world. There is no tree of life anywhere. We take the bark of this plant; we grind another up; we cherish the early seeds of yet another; we take their fruits and nuts and use them to halt some of our most vicious cancers and neurological disorders. And sometime they work, like the root from Issyk Kul that helped Solzhenitsyn destroy his malignancy. But there is no single plant that can guarantee that, once we eat it, we will live forever. Right?

Wrong. There is one; in fact, it is the very tree of life appearing once again. Revelation 2 talks of it when it reprimands the Ephesian Christians for forsaking their first love. It urges them to repent and return to their zealous former life of enthusiastic discipleship. Then we read: "He who has an ear, let him hear what the Spirit says to the churches. To him who overcomes, I will give the right to eat from the tree of life which is in the paradise of God" (v. 7; see also 22:2, 19).

People who know they are going to live forever through the victory of Jesus Christ know that the day is coming when the menace of the flaming cherubim sword will be gone. Instead, the guardians of the tree of life will bow at the waist and turn the point of their sword toward the splendid tree and invite the victors to eat and live forever.

So we travel between two life-giving trees, the one whose blessing we have forfeited, the other whose blessing will sustain us forevermore—the tree of life in the paradise of God.

Thank you, O Lord God, for telling us of the tree of life in the new paradise. We look with eagerness toward the day when the curse on our poor lives will be removed and we can eat freely of its life-giving fruit. In Jesus' name, Amen.

SEVEN

The Covenant Connection

"You must not eat of the tree of the knowledge of good and evil, for when you eat of it you will surely die."
—Genesis 2:17

Long-time Christians often form deep and emotional attachments to certain words and sounds, even if they are not able to tell you exactly what the words and sounds really mean. I believe it was Mark Twain who wrote about a woman who loved to go to church because she loved the sounds of the words, especially the word *Mesopotamia*. It gave her goose bumps.

Covenant is such a word. It makes people feel good to hear it once in awhile. Sometimes they even include the word in the names of their churches. But when cornered, they don't know exactly what it means.

A man who helped me understand the meaning of *covenant* was Herman Bavinck, a theologian who died in 1921. He said this: "Among rational and moral creatures all higher life takes the form of a covenant. Generally, a covenant is an agreement between persons who voluntarily obligate and bind themselves to each other for the purpose of fending off an evil or obtaining a good. Such an agreement [whether explicitly stated or assumed] is the usual form in terms of which humans live and work together. Love, friendship, marriage, as well as all social cooperation in business, industry, science, art . . . is [sic] ultimately grounded in a covenant, that is, in reciprocal fidelity and an assortment of generally recognized moral obligations" (Herman Bavinck, *In the Beginning*, John Bolt, ed., Baker, 1999, p. 203).

Well, that's a mouthful, but it surely makes a lot of sense. It's true, isn't it, that our significant human relationships are covenantal. We have no such relationship with the check-out person in the supermarket, but as soon as we make a deal with a roofer to put a new roof on our house, we have a covenant going: you do this, I'll pay you; you fail, and you won't get paid. Marriage is the most significant covenant relationship many of us have during our lives. But parents and children have a covenant relationship too: you do this and that, and we, your parents, will take care of you—but if you are disobedient, we'll have to take another look at our relationship.

The great message of the Bible is that God enters into a covenant relationship with his people. God says, "I will be your God if you obey me"; of course, God being God, we cannot turn to him and lay down conditions God must fulfill. When God says he will be our God if we obey him, he means that he will be our protector, our friend, and the supplier of our every need while we are in this world. And he will glorify us throughout all eternity.

We find this at the very beginning of the Bible. After creating human beings in his image, God approached Adam, who not only represented all human beings who were to come later, but was at that time the entire human race, and laid out the covenant to him. I would like to think that they had a perfect relationship, but it wasn't entirely perfect—after all, Adam was able to fall into sin, though he had not yet done so. In any case, it was a marvelously beautiful and satisfying relationship for both God and Adam. Just to think of what that must have been like sets our heads spinning. But human obedience was the key; therefore, God created a situation of probation and commanded Adam not to eat of the tree of the knowledge of good and evil.

It's true: *covenant* is an unusually important word. We have to understand it if we are going to understand our relationship to God. The word itself is not found in Genesis 2, where we read of the way God put Adam on probation to test him to see if he would be obedient. However, Hosea 6:7 refers back to the command God gave Adam in the Garden of Eden, calling it a covenant. And Bavinck insists this is a covenant relationship: "The command given to Adam was . . . a covenant because it was intended, like God's covenant with Israel, to convey eternal life to Adam in the way of [covenantal] obedience" (*In the Beginning*, p. 199).

Today, God enters into a relationship of covenantal love with those who believe in Jesus Christ, who is the last, or second, Adam—he is the one whose perfect obedience restores our relationship with our covenant God. Oh, how he loves you and me!

Almighty God, as we realize that you have entered into covenant with your people and still do today, we praise you for your amazing love. We, like Adam, are often disobedient. Thank you for receiving us in Jesus, who now is our covenant representative. Hear us in his name, Amen.

EIGHT

Covenant Breakers

"He will crush your head, and you will strike his heel."
—Genesis 3:15

I t's encouraging to think of ourselves as eternal people, but it's going to be a horrible eternity in hell unless God does something to repair the damage we caused when we broke the covenant.

When our first parents stood outside the gates of paradise, embarrassed beyond words because of their nakedness and their pathetic attempt to cover it, they were miserable. Their little minds were going top speed trying to put a spin on what had happened that would get them off the hook. But it didn't work. Adam had no one to blame but himself. He had heard God's command and understood it. What he didn't understand was that the death God talked about was worse than the death of any animal—it was separation from God. From God!

There is much in the Bible that we can imagine and comprehend to some degree. But this is a scene that falls outside our ability to do either: when Adam ate the forbidden fruit Eve offered him, he destroyed the covenant relationship he had with God. In the first moments of his transgression, he may not have realized the gravity of his rebellion, but by the time he stood with Eve outside Eden's gate, there was no avoiding the implications of what he had done.

From the moment of that first sin, the only hope for Adam and his children lay with God. Even in the state of integrity, before he fell, the creature Adam was not on par with the Creator God. With his disobedience, the tollgate slammed down and the way between Adam and God was barred. From then on it would be only the kind favor of God that would remove the barrier and make it possible for humanity to enjoy a blessed covenant relationship with God again.

Right there, where sentry cherubim stood resolute guard and a fiery sword flashed back and forth, God began to respond to humankind with his grace. From that day forward the covenant based on Adam's obedience would have to be adjusted so that the very keeping of the covenant would ultimately have to be accomplished by God himself. And God would have to right the horrendous wrong that had been perpetrated by our race. Payment would have to be made for Adam's sin . . . and Eve's . . . and ours.

Our first parents likely did not look that much different from the way they'd looked the day before the Fall, but they stood before God, who had become their judge, helplessly and hopelessly. Without divine intervention, the path they walked led inexorably to hell. So God moved in and announced that someone would finally come who would experience terrifying punishment but who would, finally, crush the serpent's head.

God's covenant dealings with his people continued, but the first covenant, which required Adam's obedience, would have to give way to another way of accomplishing what it was designed to do. The first expression of God's covenant mercy was designed to insure that God and humanity would walk together through the corridors of history and forever. Now Adam was crippled. It would be impossible to achieve the goals of that first covenant through human performance of any kind.

So the covenant of grace was put in place; standing east of Eden, we see the first hints of what it would ultimately become. God himself would become Eve's offspring in the person of Jesus Christ, and God would pay the penalty and be obedient fully to the will of God. What Adam failed to do, Christ would do perfectly.

Surely Adam, already vitiated by sin and dazed by the presence of God and the divine curses that fell on the earth, on those around him, and on himself, did not grasp the meaning of God's promise of a Savior who would crush the serpent's head. But he did understand what was happening when, after the cursing, God himself made garments of skins. If he had never seen an animal die before, he saw it then, as God did whatever was necessary to clothe these pitiable people.

Blood had to be shed to cover the nakedness of our cowering parents. In time the precious blood of Christ would be shed to cover Adam's iniquities and ours. There, where ruined people stood among the shambles of a ruined world, we see the first intimations of something more beautiful than the garden at its best: grace appeared. Grace will repair the ruin. God's grace.

Grace *is* amazing.

O God, as we have remembered how we brought ruin to your splendid creation, we hang our heads in shame. And we are so thankful for your amazing grace. Please cover our wretched shame with Christ's righteous robes. In his name, Amen.

NINE

Faith and Walking

Anyone who comes to [God] must believe that he exists
and that he rewards those who earnestly seek him.
—Hebrews 11:6

F*aith* is a funny word. It's as bad as *love:* it means all sorts of things in peoples' minds. Everyone has faith of one kind or another. Atheists have to have faith in themselves, otherwise they wouldn't believe themselves when they claim that no god exists.

Christians keep saying that we are saved by faith, but what if those who hear have an idea of faith that doesn't square with the Bible? Then we might as well tell them they can be saved by eating pizza.

Hebrews 11 tells us how we can spot saving faith when it gives brief bullets on the lives of certain characters who appear on the Old Testament's pages. Genesis 5 tells us about Enoch; the details are sparse but intriguing. He "walked" with God. And one day God said to him, "Enoch, enough of this walking together here, come on home." Hebrews 11 says that Enoch never died. According to Genesis 5, "He was no more, because God took him away" (v. 24).

We should think about Enoch more, and we should be jealous. Trouble is, most of us don't really want to walk with God the way Enoch did. You walk with someone, and pretty soon you find yourself telling that person some of your inmost thoughts. If you walk together long enough, after a while you start thinking like your walk mate.

Enoch had the right kind of faith. Immediately after talking about Enoch, Hebrews 11 tells us what kind of faith pleases God. Notice two things about such faith: it believes that God exists, and it believes that God rewards those who earnestly seek him.

24

Now, this is not the standard definition; in fact, because it talks about reward, it seems to contradict the notion that we are saved by grace alone, not by works. Even so, let's look at it for a moment—it's obviously an important description of faith since it describes the faith that enabled Enoch to escape the grave.

Number one, good faith—the kind that pleases God—is certainty that the true God, who is revealed in the Bible, is the true God. Of course, Enoch didn't have a Bible. But he had God's special revelation. Even before Moses arrived on the scene, the message had been kept alive. I believe that Enoch knew about Adam, and he knew about the promise that God made to our cringing parents outside the gates of paradise, the promise that someone was coming who would destroy the serpent. Enoch knew he was walking with the God who made the heavens and the earth. His days were consumed by his passion to be with God, to think about God, and, who knows, possibly to receive messages from God.

We have to realize that Enoch was in touch with the true God. Faith in other gods is worse than no faith at all. So today we walk with God when we live out of the revelation God has given us, now full and complete. We find it in the Scripture, but mainly we find it in his only Son, Jesus Christ, about whom we learn when we study the Bible.

Granted—I have heard that a thousand times. But true faith is confidence that this true God rewards those who earnestly seek him. This makes faith very practical. God responds to his people. God is a personal being who created our race so that he could communicate with us and we with him. The Old Testament is about God's contact with his people, who prayed to him and wept copious tears in his presence. One of the prophets told the Israelites, "Seek the Lord while he may be found. . . . " Seek him. Seek him.

When we earnestly seek him, we find him. Jesus himself said, "Seek and you will find."

Everything God has done, he has done so that boys and girls and men and women of faith will seek him . . . earnestly. When they do, God responds to them.

Now we know that we cannot even seek God unless God seeks us first, and we know that the reward God gives is not of merit but of grace. True enough. But it all boils down to this: true faith is expressed when ordinary sinners seek God earnestly and find him.

True faith results in walking with God. Walking. Not running. Walking.

O Lord, maker of heaven and earth, divine lover of your needy people,
help me seek you as Enoch did. Lord, I want to walk with you.
Please. I pray in Christ's name, Amen.

TEN

Father Abraham

Abram believed the LORD, and he credited it to him as righteousness.
—Genesis 15:6

The time span between the Fall and Abram's appearance on the scene is difficult to reckon as to length, and it is full of events that stir our curiosity but do not satisfy it. We know about Enoch and Methuselah and learn about the flood and the tower of Babel, but not until we come to Abraham do we enter a time we can understand. This man lived 2,000 years before Christ, just as we live 2,000 years after him.

Abraham—to use the name God eventually gave him—emerges as a powerful figure, shrewd and determined, often sinful. With him, however, the form of God's new covenant with his chosen people takes recognizable shape. Choosing Abraham's offspring as his special people and making them his treasured possession was God's response to the destruction Adam brought upon the earth with his disobedience.

In the covenant God made with Abraham, faith was of primary importance. In Genesis 15 God repeats the promise made to Abraham earlier in Genesis 12—a promise of nationhood. Abraham would become a nation that would ultimately embrace all sorts of people; he would become a blessing to the entire earth.

To those of us who have studied the Bible for many years, this covenant promise does not seem surprising because we have heard it so often. For Abraham, however, this divine statement had no support whatsoever in the circumstances that surrounded him. He heard it first in Ur of the Chaldeans, a bustling city with multistoried buildings—a virtual Chicago—and in obedience to God's marching orders he moved across the desert to Haran, where his father, still an idolater, had died. From there, he traveled south to the big tree of Moreh at Shechem, where the Lord told him that he would give the entire land we know as Canaan to him. It was a preposterous idea, something like receiving a big envelope telling you that you have won the sweepstakes.

Abraham was not dumb, and he could see that what God had promised was absurd. The primary barrier in the way to his becoming a nation was simply this: to become a nation, you need to have children, and he had none. Sarah, his dear wife, now ninety years of age, was, to say the least, not fecund. Some days, he would look over at Eliezer, his executive assistant, a nice enough fellow, but hardly a person he wanted for his heir. Did God have this man in mind when he promised Abraham the land he had just traveled through?

In the face of all these problems God promised Abraham the impossible. God told Abraham to forget Eliezer and then assured him, "A son coming from your own body will be your heir" (v. 4). Then the maker of the universe directed Abraham's attention heavenward, where countless stars spangled the moonless night. "Count them if you can," God said. "You're looking at your family, Abraham; that's how many children you will have."

Christians who have heard this story 250 times do not realize what it must have been like the night the covenant promise was expressed so clearly. We whose faith is supported by great music and by preaching and the reading of Scripture (to say nothing of the social side of being a Christian—potluck suppers and all) must understand the significance of what happened when Abraham took God at his word. There were no props that moonless night, just the promise. After it was spoken, all the barriers to its fulfillment still remained. But, the Bible says, Abraham believed the Lord.

From that night on, God considered Abraham righteous, sinner though he was. Once again, we see the shape of the covenant. We cannot create our righteousness with our deeds, but when we believe, God considers us righteous.

It is the same today when we stand alone with God in the dark night. God speaks to us and tells us that he will be our God every step of our journey, and someday he will take us into glory. Christ has gone before. We believe he is God's Son, and we believe that he died to pay for all our sin. Together we say the creed of the Apostles: *I believe in the forgiveness of sin, the resurrection of the body and life everlasting.* Impossible. But those who believe it today are righteous along with Father Abraham, no matter what their nation. They are the children God talked with him about so many years ago.

Sovereign God, as we remember that righteousness comes through faith in you, we remember too that we cannot have this faith unless you put it in our hearts. Make our faith strong in this day and make us happy because we are stars in Abraham's sky—we are his children. In Christ, Amen.

ELEVEN

Faith = Obedience

Then he reached out his hand and took the knife to slay his son.
—Genesis 22:10

Unless a person wants his life to be totally changed, it would be foolish for him to reach out for true, saving faith. Contrary to the usual descriptions of how nice faith is, the truth is that once it is established in a person's life, it turns into a fierce, uncompromising master. Once you truly believe in God and in his Son Jesus Christ as your Savior, you will become involved in events you would have avoided if left to yourself.

You can spell faith two ways: the usual way—*f a i t h*—and this way—*o b e d i e n c e*. Faith and obedience are actually equivalent terms. Writing to the Romans, the apostle Paul said that he had received the task to call people "to the obedience that comes from faith" (Rom. 1:5).

When God enters into a covenant relationship with people he tests them. He disciplines them to determine how genuine their faith is and to make them stronger. "Endure hardship as discipline; God is treating you as sons" (Heb. 12:7).

Abraham discovered what happens when faith moves out of the realm of the theoretical into the reality of life. In Genesis 22 God called Abraham, and Abraham responded with his usual "Here I am." Then he heard words that filled him with horror and revulsion: "Take your son, your only son, Isaac, whom you love, and go to the region of Moriah. Sacrifice him there as a burnt offering on one of the mountains I will tell you about" (v. 2).

Abraham obeyed . . . at once. Early the next morning, he set out for Moriah with two of his servants and Isaac. Before leaving their camp, they collected the wood for the burnt offering; Isaac likely helped. Abraham trembled within as he struggled with his emotions. Then, at the foot of the designated mountain, he and Isaac left the servants and scrambled up the mountain together. Abraham carried the knife and the fire; Isaac carried the wood.

It was a very puzzled young boy who finally asked the obvious question: "Dad, aren't you forgetting something? Where is the lamb for the sacrifice?" The question fell like a stone along the mountain path. Abraham spoke: "God himself will provide the lamb for the burnt offering, my son."

The Genesis chapter continues to supply each chilling detail. When they reached the place of offering, Abraham constructed the altar, bringing some stones and clods of earth together to form a raised mound. He arranged the wood, and then . . . then, he took the son he loved, the son named laughter (for that is what *Isaac* means), the son through whom God had promised to fulfill the covenant. He took him and, using the same rope that had bound the wood, bound Isaac securely, and laid him—*laid him*—on the wood.

There was only one thing left to do before he would use the fire he carried to ignite the altar's wood. He would have to kill Isaac, just as he had killed so many cattle, sheep, and rams. He looked at Isaac; he felt the knife, heavy in his hand. He would plunge the knife into his son's heart so that death would come instantly. He took a deep breath and raised his hand. Isaac's eyes were wide with horror. His mouth opened, and he was about to shriek. But the next sound they heard was God's voice—Abraham's name, repeated twice, resounded along the mountain ridge.

"Do not lay a hand on the boy. . . . Do not do anything to him. Now I know that you fear God, because you have not withheld from me your son, your only son." And then God provided a ram to take Isaac's place.

When we look at this episode in the light of the entire Bible, we see the foreshadowing of the day when God would give his dearly beloved Son for the salvation of his people. Now let us just note this: God tests the faith of the faithful. Hebrews 11 presents what happened here as the supreme guarantee that Abraham's faith was genuine. "Abraham reasoned that God could raise the dead, and figuratively speaking, he did receive Isaac back from death" (v. 19).

Abraham believed God totally, absolutely, without reservation. When God tested him, he obeyed. So must we. We must obey.

God of Abraham, we know you have tested us and you will test us again. Make us obedient. Make us willing to do whatever you ask of us. Give us the kind of faith that is obedient. No other kind makes any difference. In Christ, Amen.

TWELVE

Driven by Faith.

By faith Abraham . . . obeyed and went,
even though he did not know where he was going.
—Hebrews 11:8

The last thing we think of when we think of faith is high motivation. Many consider faith the refuge of lazy minds or an intriguing embellishment of life or the cause of no end of problems. In the Bible, though, true, saving faith is an engine that drives people relentlessly.

On the Bible's pages, ancient Abraham, who walked this planet about 4,000 years ago, emerges as the prototype believer, a person we must examine closely if we are to know how we should live. The dominant word the Bible uses to describe him is *faithful.* But he was not a man of quiet contemplation; rather, his faith drove him along uncharted paths. People who have true faith are men and women of action.

It was a life-jolting switch from the citified ambience of Ur of the Chaldeans to the nomadic life Abraham adopted at God's command. God told him to journey into the unknown, and Abraham obeyed.

All those whom we have come to call "heroes of faith" in Hebrews 11 were men and women who did something courageous because they believed what God told them. Each of them is described as a person who believed in the true God and consequently did something heroic. Whether or not we do something heroic for God proves the authenticity of our faith.

Of all the heroes in Hebrews 11, Abraham dominates; he is the one who shows the way faith-filled people live. "By faith Abraham, when called to go to a place he would later receive as his inheritance, obeyed and went, even though he did not know where he was going. By faith he made his home in the promised land like a stranger in a foreign country; he lived in tents, as did Isaac and Jacob, who were heirs with him of the same promise" (vv. 9-10).

Yes, Abraham was a driven man, as much so as the most driven business tycoon, the most dedicated athlete, the greediest financier. When he finally arrived in the promised land, he was very vulnerable, swinging in the wind, with enemies looking down at him from the heights. The place was strange and unknown, with cities here and there that gave off the putrid odor of depravity. Abraham came because God had told him that this land would be his, a preposterous idea by any measure. But he believed, and he obeyed.

Faith has a present element: Hebrews 11 opens with the statement that faith tells us something about creation: "By faith we understand that the universe was formed at God's command, so that what is seen was not made out of what was visible" (v. 3). And faith has a future focus: Abraham was "looking toward the city with foundations, whose architect and builder is God" (v. 10).

God is an architect and a builder. Just let your eyes roam over the plains and the mountains, Abraham, says God, and lie stunned in the night as you see the stars in the sky. Abraham knew that the God who talked to him was the same one who had made all these things. And someday, he knew, this same architect would perfectly construct a holy, eternal city. Hundreds of thousands of people would live within that future city in perfect holiness and peace.

Once God establishes true faith in a person's soul, that faith becomes the driving power that affects what that person does every day. When God told Abraham to leave, the Bible says, "he obeyed." All of us are driven by some vision, an inner force, a power that directs our efforts toward a goal. Those who earnestly want to be Christians must examine their lives carefully and discover what it is that is driving them. Is it the relentless acquisition of more and more things, which we see all around us, or is it the commands of God?

Believers are driven people. They follow Christ now; and as they look around the next bend in the road, as they look beyond the horizon, they see a glorious future.

O God, what is driving me? What is motivating me? I confess to you now that it is not my faith all the time. I want to live by faith as Abraham did. Keep before me the eternal glory you promise believers. May I be driven in all I do today by my desire to obey you, O Lord. I pray in Christ's name, Amen.

THIRTEEN

Who Goes to Heaven?

If you belong to Christ, then you are Abraham's seed,
and heirs according to the promise.
—Galatians 3:29

Who is going to make it into heaven? Most of us have some interest in the answer to this question. The answer is really quite astonishing and specific in the Bible: *Abraham's children are going to make it into heaven.* No one else? So far as we can tell from the Bible, *no one else.*

That's not the usual answer, is it? If you read the book of Galatians in the New Testament, you discover that it's Abraham's children all the way. Isn't it strange that this man, who lived 2000 years before Galatians was written, pops up on its pages? But there he is; read chapter 3 and you'll find that he is the main character. The chapter concludes with this unexpected statement about Abraham's children.

What's going on here?

First of all, we have to realize that Abraham is the person who demonstrated what saving faith is. In Galatians 3:6, there's a reference to Genesis 15:6, where we learn that Abraham believed God and "he credited it to him as righteousness." Only those whom God considers righteous are going to make it into heaven, and since not one of us is righteous, there has to be a way, outside ourselves, to become righteous. Abraham showed what that way was and still is today. When people believe God's promise, God mercifully credits them with a righteousness he gives them, not a righteousness they have created themselves.

Today, believers do the same thing Abraham did. One man, scared out of his wits, asked the apostle Paul: "What must I do to be saved?" Paul replied, "Believe in the Lord Jesus and you will be saved" (Acts 16:30-31). That's the way it is today. Believers believe in the Lord Jesus Christ for their salvation. They believe that his death paid for their sin and that they will live eternally with him. These are the promises of God—promises that are even greater than the promises God gave Abraham. When we believe God's promise of realities that seem like impossibilities in our view, God considers us righteous.

So Abraham's children are those who take God at his word just as Abraham did. And only Abraham's children will go to heaven.

Second, when we think about Abraham's children, we are required to leap into a way of thinking totally different from our usual way of thinking about race. Abraham was the father of the Jewish nation. The Jews of Jesus' day proudly declared, "We are Abraham's descendants and have never been slaves of anyone" (John 8:33). So they spoke, and so they lived. Today, however, the idea *Abraham's children* has nothing to do with race, nothing to do with social status, nothing to do with gender. But it has everything to do with Christ. People qualify as Abraham's children if they have faith in Jesus Christ—if they believe the promises of God that he made in Christ.

Remember how, when God promised Abraham he would be the father of many nations, he took him outside his tent on a dark night and showed him the stars. No one can count the stars. God said that Abraham's children would be like the stars of the sky in number. That was God's promise to an aged, childless man whose wife was barren. Abraham believed that promise, but he had no idea how it would be fulfilled. Now we know how that promise is being fulfilled. Being a child of Abraham has nothing to do with being Jewish; it has everything to do with believing that Christ is your Savior. Believers in Christ are Abraham's children. The promise made beneath the stars has come true as billions of people of all the nations of the earth have believed and are believing in Christ.

The apostle Paul said it best: "Understand, then, that those who believe are children of Abraham. The Scripture foresaw that God would justify the Gentiles by faith, and announced the gospel in advance to Abraham: 'All nations will be blessed through you.' So those who have faith are blessed along with Abraham, the man of faith" (Gal. 3:7-9).

Many Jews today believe in Christ and have become spiritual sons and daughters of Abraham through their faith. And all the rest of us believers grin as we say to them: Move over Judah and Deborah, and make room for us Gentiles; we are children of Abraham too. And all of us are going to spend a wonderful eternity together.

O Sovereign God, how majestic are your ways! They are past finding out.
Help us believe that your promises never fail. Your promises to Abraham
have not failed, and we know that your promise of eternal life
in Jesus will not fail either. In his name, Amen.

FOURTEEN

Wendy's Family

The LORD . . . has chosen you out of all the peoples . . .
of the earth to be his people, his treasured possession.
—Deuteronomy 7:6

When I talked with Wendy, I was surprised to hear that she was planning to move. I had been in her condo for a meeting and was impressed with how commodious it was and how tastefully decorated. It was in the Hyde Park area of Chicago, near the university where she was working on her dissertation. Seemed to be plenty of room for the three of them: her husband, an engineer; three-year-old Bethany; and herself. Why move?

She explained that they were thinking of Bethany's schooling and the schooling of any other children they might be given. She said that she wanted to be part of a covenant community that would help her educate her children. Something like that was starting up in Chicago's south side, in the Beverley section—so that's where they were going to go. They were planning to enroll Bethany at the Covenant Christian Academy. And, she said, they were trying to convince other young families like themselves to move to the same area so that they could experience community together.

It fascinated me that this young woman understood something that many Christians these days seem to have missed. When we live in the light of the Scripture—the entire Scripture, both Old and New Testament—we learn that God expects that his people will dwell in community; they will "clump together." The idea of "the people of God" dominates both Old and New Testament.

Virtually nothing is addressed to solitary Christians in the Scriptures. Everything about the Bible presupposes that the people of God live together, help one another, and, as Wendy clearly saw, educate their children together. The Old Testament describes believers as a group who lived together in the same geographical setting, worshiped together, worked together, and helped one another so that no one would be poor. And in the New Testament, virtually all of the books are addressed to large groups of people, not just to single individuals. This is true even of the gospel of Luke and the book of Acts, which were written for Theophilis; as we read them we realize that they were actually written for the people of God—living together, believing together.

When I heard Wendy's vision of community, I was encouraged. She and others like her tell me that young people these days are earnestly seeking the experience of community. In some cases, these young adults don't even know what they are missing, but as soon as someone suggests to them that what they really need is community—true fellowship with a broader family of men, women, and children—their eyes light up. "Why yes, that's what I have been missing; that's exactly what I need," they're likely to say.

So much in our culture drives people away from each other—powerful, centrifugal forces—that we need the Doppler effect to figure out where our family and friends have gone. Advancing technology is taking its toll. People become prisoners in their condos and apartments, buying their goods on the Internet and having their groceries delivered by Peapod.com. Chat rooms, websites, working in cyberspace in a virtual office at home—such activities are causing isolation, according to Stanford professor Norman H. Nie. More than a third of those who responded to his study said they thought the hours spent on the Internet were causing them to interact less with family members and friends. Real relationships with real human beings are diminishing these days.

And the church itself often fails to emphasize that once we believe in Christ, we need other Christians. We have brothers and sisters. We need to be willing to make moves, even geographical moves, so that we will be close enough to one another to help each other and to educate our God-given children together.

Wendy realized that her family needed to be part of this bigger family—God's family, this treasured possession, which God has chosen from all the peoples on the face of the earth.

When we live in the light of eternity, with ideals that affect our eternal experience, we may not try to be a Christian all by ourselves. We need each other. We need the community—the bigger family—and our children need this community too.

Almighty God, as we believe in you may we see beyond ourselves to the greater community of those who believe as we do. Be with those who have to make a move to another place to experience your covenant people, and help them do it. In Jesus' name, Amen.

FIFTEEN

The Inheritance We Share

"Here am I, and the children God has given me."
—Hebrews 2:13

W hen Jesus' disciples approached him, requesting instruction in prayer, the last thing they probably thought would happen was that Jesus would tell them to address God as *Father*. That just wasn't part of their vocabulary for talking to God. To be sure, the Old Testament gives hints of God's fatherhood, but there are no instances, as far as I know, in which people had the boldness to address God as their father. (Psalm 89:26 comes close but it doesn't really do so.) When the Jewish people thought about any kind of a father beyond their own, they thought about Father Abraham.

Here is another instance of familiarity blinding us: because we have thought about God as our Father for so long, the sheer wonder of it has worn away. But it is astonishing beyond words that we can address God this way.

Let's be honest about this. It may be true that God is our Father in the sense that God is the origin of everything we are. We are his children, yes; but my, oh my, have we made a mess of our lives! We are like the prodigal son who came home after spending his father's inheritance with whores at bars and said, "Father, I have sinned against heaven and against you. I am no longer worthy to be called your son . . . " (Luke 15:18-19).

Jesus knows all these sordid details. Yet he teaches us to call God "our Father" when we pray. How come?

What we must underscore here is the word *our*. None of us may approach God using this address all by ourselves. We must do so in the company of Jesus Christ. Father God is not just *my* Father; he's *our* Father. When Jesus told us to address God as "our Father," he had in mind that we would do so with his arm across our shoulder.

Christ Jesus has been God's Son forever and will forever be his Son. The Son has been eternally born of the Father—always has been and always will be. The book of Hebrews opens by emphasizing the way Christ Jesus is "the radiance of God's glory and the exact representation of his being" (1:3).

And Hebrews emphasizes that this glorious Son of God appears before God in the company of his children. He keeps saying to his Father in heaven, "Here am I, and the children God has given me." Is Jesus saying here that we are his children? Could be. But more likely, he is saying to his heavenly Father that these are the Father's children, and they have been given to Jesus. Jesus is God's Son, and believers, through Jesus' life and death and resurrection, become God's children too, with Jesus as their exalted brother.

So we speak to God when we pray, "Our Father . . . " We come into our Father's presence in this blessed association. It's as if God says to us, "Any friend of Jesus is a friend of mine," except that God says it on a far deeper level. Our Father actually says, "Any friend of Jesus is my child, just as Jesus is."

Christ Jesus continuously presents his children to his Father in heaven. He is like the proud leader of a grade school choir who, at the end of a surprisingly grand concert, steps aside, bows to the proud parents, extends her arm toward the beaming choristers, and declares by her gesture: Yes, these are the children you have given me.

So we pray to "our Father"—Jesus' Father and ours through faith in Jesus. Every time God the Father sees us he sees his Son. And every time he sees his Son, he sees us.

I must confess that when I have addressed God as "our Father" over the years, I have not usually thought about all that is involved in calling God by this name. We learn to call God "our Father" when we are young children, and we don't have a clue about what it means. As we grow older, we seldom take the time to reflect on the depth of meaning in this simple address to the divine. Because we think of this seldom, if ever, we miss the wonder and the certainty that we are eternal creatures.

Surely, anyone who can address almighty God with such a term is elevated thereby to the highest level of existence. A person who is God's child because of faith in God's blessed Son will have a blessed experience in the present—today— and that experience will never end.

O God, my Father, help me think about these things when I pray.
Overwhelm me with the wonder of what it means to talk to you
in the company of the Son you love. Receive me, heavenly Father,
as your Son presents me to you just now. Amen.

SIXTEEN

Behind Closed Doors

"Go into your room, close the door, and pray to your Father. . . . "
—Matthew 6:6

When the door closes and you are alone with your heavenly Father, what happens?

That depends.

There are days when you are simply quiet, even confused, as you begin your time in God's presence. You need time to adjust to the quietness that surrounds you. Possibly you need a few minutes to become fully awake if it is early in the morning. Maybe you need to compose your thoughts because you have just been arguing, or you may have just read something that disturbs you or seen something on television that has driven you far from your Father's home. But now it is time. It is the time you set aside to be with your Father, alone. You are there once again, and the door is closed.

"Close the door." When Jesus said that, he was not declaring that only "behind-closed-doors" prayer is authentic. Sometimes in church we are led by someone else in prayer, and we feel our heads nodding as he or she speaks to God about concerns that are close to our own hearts; sometimes we join others in a prayer time and each one prays as led. But Jesus wants us to know that prayer in the fullest sense occurs when just one Christian, alone, meets with God privately, even secretly. The closed door emphasizes that prayer in the first degree is nonpublic.

Jesus often observed those who like to pray in public; usually Pharisees with their distinctive dress, blue tassels long and obvious, standing on the street corner where everyone could see them at the hour of prayer. Or he would see them in the temple, as close to God as they could get, lifting up their voices as they thanked God that they were not like other men . . . and that they were not women. Jesus knew that their prayers were getting nowhere; they literally vanished into thin air. Those public prayers were a sham. Only their audience took note of them and honored these dramatic religious leaders accordingly. That was their only reward. "Don't get into that bag," Jesus said. "Pray by yourself behind closed doors and talk to your Father in heaven there." Secret, private prayers don't vanish; they make it all the way to heaven's throne room.

But what does happen when the door closes? Sometimes we spill our guts in agony to God. Mirth Vos, for example, did that. Vos was a psychotherapist who often told her clients to journal; she would coach them as they painstakingly noted the swings in their emotions. When, after fourteen years of battling cancer, she was finally told, "There is nothing we can do for you, but we will make you comfortable," she was plunged into anguish. Some weeks before writing this, I was one of six who carried her coffin to the grave on a bitter cold day outside Barrie, Ontario. But before she died, she left her own journal. That journal, published as *Letters to Myself on Dying*, is part of the legacy she left behind.

Mirth was like Jacob wrestling with God on Jabbock's shore; she held up his holy Word and waved it before her heavenly Father. She poured out her heart in the early morning, by herself, in the holy place. She was like the writer of Psalm 63: "O God, you are my God, earnestly I seek you; my soul thirsts for you, my body longs for you in a dry and weary land where there is no water. . . . " Her Father heard her cries and he rewarded her; the last words I heard from her lips were simple ones: "I want just to fade away . . . into the arms of Jesus."

Confusion, sometimes weeping, crying out to God, sometimes meditating, sometimes mulling over Jesus' perfect prayer, praising him, beseeching him, interceding—these activities take place when the door slips shut and we are alone. The secret place of prayer is often not a scene of calm and peace. Sometimes events in our lives shatter us and make us angry, even angry with God. But there, behind the closed door, life is renewed and the beginning of joy is restored . . . at least the beginning.

"Master, teach us to pray," the disciples requested, and Jesus began by telling them where to pray. Not there on the street corner where you will be observed, but in that place where no one will notice. That is the place. Those who find that place and frequent it daily will be rewarded with the Father's reward, the only reward that carries over into glory.

Heavenly Father, bring me daily to the secret place of prayer. Please understand that there are days when I do better in your presence than other days. Holy Spirit, help me when the door slips closed. For Jesus' sake, Amen.

SEVENTEEN

Our Father?

"Our Father in heaven, hallowed be your name. . . . "
—Matthew 6:9

I f we were really to take Jesus seriously when he teaches us to pray, we might pray more often than we do. Unfortunately, we know the perfect prayer so well and we have said it so often that it has ceased to astonish us. But there it is, right at the beginning—Jesus tells us to call God "our Father."

This is a mind-boggling revelation: God is our Father. To be sure, the Bible describes God in terms that make us keep our distance: "God, the blessed and only Ruler, the King of kings and Lord of lords, who alone is immortal and who lives in unapproachable light, whom no one has seen or can see" (1 Tim. 6:15-16).

What would you ever say if you stumbled into the presence of such a being? We must remember that Jesus is talking about the same being when he teaches us to pray. The "unapproachable light" is real enough, but Jesus says that when we go into our prayer room and close the door, we may begin our conversation by calling the one who dwells in this dazzling light *Father*.

We should try to figure out what Jesus had in mind when he told us to talk to God this way. What was he thinking of?

Shouldn't we start by remembering that Jesus was deeply aware of what happened when God created us? God is our Father because God created us. My Father is my father in a similar way. According to the Bible, every person is in this world because of his father's will. It may have been a wretchedly evil will, expressed in the hideous passion of a rapist, but it was a father's initiative nonetheless. Thankfully, most children are begotten by fathers considerably more honorable and committed, but always the will of a father is the decisive factor in every person's life.

When we pray, we may remember that the person we address is the one responsible for our being here. When we speak to God, he is delighted, as a father is delighted when his child, just three months old, smiles at him and makes those sounds that are the beginning of speech.

Those who have been Christians for a long time and who know a little about how Christ has redeemed them are apt to forget that the first thing about calling God our Father is the simple fact that he is our father in the ordinary sense of that term. Surely he was Adam's father, and Eve's—he made them from the dust of the earth and breathed into them and they became living beings. They were the products of his artifice. And we have come from those people. God made them and God made us.

And then, God made us when he controlled the incredible potentiality that resides in our genetics. Ask Francis Collins about the Genome Project, and you will discover what has gone into making you who you are. Consider this quote from the Associated Press: "The human genetic pattern, or genome, is a biological map laying out the sequence of 3 billion pairs of chemicals that make up the DNA in each cell. All human DNA is contained within 23 pairs of chromosomes." Collins, who heads the international project that has already completed the draft copy of our gene catalogue, is a Christian; I assume that he would agree that we may believe that God put each of us together. Our genetic structure is not the result of the flip of a cosmic coin; it's the result of "designer genes." The psalmist said it beautifully: "O LORD . . . you knit me together in my mother's womb" (Ps. 139:13).

When Jesus encourages us to go to the God of God, Light of light, and begin by addressing him as Father, he reminds us of our origin. No matter how far we may be estranged from God—by neglect, by bondage to certain sins, by simply not ever having learned much about him—when we pray to him, it is not like two strangers meeting for the first time in Cleveland. We build on a rich, most intimate history: we are speaking to the one who made us and determined the characteristics of our physical, emotional, and intellectual makeup.

No wonder most everyone prays to God some time or other—at least in periods of stress and horror. We have come from God's hand, after all; God's will brought us into being and made us what we are.

Each day, each hour, each moment, our Father is waiting for us to talk with him. After all, we are God's children.

O my Father, eternal God, dwelling in light unapproachable, receive my faltering prayer again this day. Forgive me for feeling so far from you. It is my fault. It is my sin. Let me never forget that I am your child. Amen.

EIGHTEEN

A Word of Caution

"Hallowed be your name. . . . "
—Matthew 6:9

P rolonged exposure to the Lord's Prayer is hazardous. To avoid the hazards, it is best to say it seldom, and when you do, to say it quickly, without thought. If you use it daily, as it is meant to be used, and consider it carefully as you say the words—if you even go so far as to make this prayer the pattern for all your prayers, you might have to call 911.

I wonder how it struck the disciples when they first heard it. I doubt if it was exactly what they had in mind. They were likely expecting that they could hasten the overthrow of the Roman rulers and reestablish the Jewish kingdom, if only they were given the right words. Probably they were baffled by Jesus' response to their request for prayer assistance.

The very first petition strikes a note that is not natural for us—we are told that we should pray that the name of the Father will be hallowed. The word *hallowed* is not one we use often, nor do we think of God's name as something that should pre-occupy our attention. But when Jesus teaches us to pray, the hallowing of God's name occupies first place.

The meaning of this petition is not particularly difficult to grasp—to hallow something is to exalt it to a place of adoration and reverence. And surely this needs tending these days, when the name of God is poured like catsup over tedious con-versations. And if you think of God's name as including the name of *Jesus* and *Christ,* it is in dire need of hallowing, considering the way these names are used profanely, often in shocking combinations with filth and sacrilege.

But seriously, if Jesus hadn't taught us this prayer, would the reverencing of God's name be our first concern as we speak to him in the early morning?

You see, the Lord's Prayer is hazardous to our ordinary lives because, over time, when used regularly and thoughtfully, it changes the way we think about life, the way we think about ourselves. When prayed with profound attention and consciousness, it gradually wears away at our usual concerns. It focuses our attention on another, higher, plane.

This prayer could ruin us. That is, it could make us of little value to an employer who rewards people only if they give him their souls in return for a six-figure salary. It could also render us somewhat odd in terms of our interests. Concern for the items the Lord's Prayer enumerates, starting with concern for reverencing God's name, could isolate us from many of the stimuli that affect others. For example, it would likely cut our television viewing down to about zero. For one thing, hearing God's name used irreverently would nauseate us; for another, once we become interested in the interests that support this prayer, a lot of the stuff that excites other people becomes terribly boring.

Those who think it's nonsense to suggest that the Lord's Prayer could change us in this way just don't get it. I'm sorry, but that is so. We have learned to use the prayer nonchalantly, virtually mindlessly, without recognizing that each word, each phrase, expresses a devastating judgment of the way we naturally are, the way we naturally think. Taking this prayer as seriously as we must assume Jesus wants us to take it, forces a total revaluation of our interests, our efforts, our goals, and our pleasures.

This prayer, after all, carries a heavenly postmark. That's where Jesus came from. It has been provided for us so that we can live as citizens of heaven, not as citizens of an earthly kingdom. This prayer is a pearl of great price, a stunning jewel that has fallen from the sky to instruct us in the most sublime and holy activity we engage in while we "travel this sod." It should be no surprise that those who use it as it should be used (repeating it often and thoughtfully and making it a pattern for all their prayers) will appear to be different from other people.

Because the prayer is otherworldly in its origin and content, it presents a hazard for those who want to be received without question within our modern society. They could well be questioned, criticized, and even scorned. And who wants that?

Lord, teach us to pray. Use the perfect prayer you've given to recreate us so that we are concerned about what you are concerned about. Help us let go of many of the ordinary concerns. And make us willing to appear somewhat strange to others. Amen.

NINETEEN

How We Hallow

"Hallowed be your name. . . . "
—Matthew 6:9

A t the time of the Protestant Reformation, when commitment to Christ was intense, people concluded that when Jesus taught them to pray that the name of his Father be hallowed, he was actually telling them to study the Bible and learn more about God.

Believers were different back then; of the millions of people who pray the Lord's Prayer today, most likely no more than 14 percent say amen and then study their Bibles because they know that that's the way we hallow God's name. But back then they had it right: if we are going to hallow God's name, we have to learn more about God.

Look at it this way.

First of all, the name of God is the most valuable, precious item we have. Just think what it would be like if we lived on this planet without knowing who made the molecules and mountains and outer space. Wouldn't this drive us batty? Think of it! To live in this marvelous creation that announces the existence of a supremely intelligent and powerful Creator without knowing who he is would be maddening.

If we want to know what happens when people live without knowing the name of God, all we have to do is look at the religions around us. When people don't know who God is, they create cruel religions or they create mystical, creepy religions. Some conclude that they themselves are gods. Those who are out of the loop of the knowledge of God are bound to do dumb things.

Second, those who realize that hallowing God's name means they need to study the Bible to learn more about him, realize that the wonderful thing about the Bible is that it tells us God's name. In fact, it tells us a number of God's names because he has several. In the Old Testament, *Jahweh* is a particularly rich name that reveals God's love for his chosen people. Other names in the Old Testament emphasize God's power and glory. And in the New Testament, the God of the Old Testament appears in *Jesus Christ,* who has been given the name that is above every name.

Now, when the Bible reveals the names of God, it does not do so in the same way that your server does when he says, "Good evening, my name is Keagan; I am your server tonight." When Keagan says that, you don't learn a single detail about his life or character. But the names of God in the Bible reveal God's character and his deeds. God's names reveal God's being. The Bible tells us who God is and what God does. That is why, once we experience the Bible as the revelation of God's name, we want to spend the rest of our lives reading and studying it.

It is not necessary for us to stumble along surrounded by God's creation but totally confused about who made it. The creation itself tells us all sorts of marvelous things about the power and divinity of God. The more we learn about it (again, think of the Genome Project, for example), the more we are astonished by God's greatness. Along with what he created, God revealed his name to us so that we could know all sorts of marvelous things about God.

When we read the Bible, we learn that God is not only powerful but also loving and gracious. Wouldn't it be horrible if the all-powerful, infinitely intelligent God who made the universe were our enemy? Wouldn't it be horrible if this great God had created us in order to play evil games with us? As we read the Bible, we learn that the truth about God is the very opposite of these horrible possibilities. God is love, and God loves the world so much that he has come here in the person of his only begotten Son to die on the cross for us.

As we live each day with our eternal destiny in mind, praying the perfect prayer and our own regular prayers with the perfect prayer as our example, there is nothing we should want more than to know more about God. We make God's name holy in our own lives as we relentlessly, joyfully, excitedly plumb the depths of the Scriptures and learn more and more about God.

Father in heaven, we thank you for revealing yourself to us. We have looked into your heart and learned that you love us unconditionally, without reservation. Help us to learn more and more and more about you. In Christ we pray, Amen.

TWENTY

Remember Me

"Your kingdom come. . . . "
— Matthew 6:10

"Jesus, remember me when you come into your kingdom."
—Luke 23:42

T here has never been a scene more ghastly. The mockery of the otherwise dig-
nified religious leaders as they paced to and fro in front of Jesus' cross was a
surreal horror. The indifference of the soldiers who crucified Jesus and then
shot craps for his clothing was macabre. The ugliness of the ordinary multitude,
who had no television violence for diversion and who were entertained by this gruesome spectacle, muttering and occasionally jeering the victims, was repulsive. And
over and through it all was a sense of death's encroachment, moving inevitably
closer as the merciless sun mounted ever higher in the heavens.

What happened on Golgotha was the opposite of what happened when God
said, "Let there be light," and there was light. This was the human race sending a
blasphemous shout toward God's throne: "Let there be darkness." And there was
darkness, unnatural and terrifying—three solid hours of it enshrouded the ghastly
scene. But before the darkness, a solitary voice showed what Jesus had in mind
when he had taught his disciples to pray "Your kingdom come."

"Jesus"—he had called him "Jesus." Nobody ever did that except the demons and
people on the fringes, like the blind man who called to him as he walked toward
Jerusalem where he would be crucified. Those who really knew him always called
him "Lord" or "Rabbi"—never "Jesus." But all the criminal had to go by was the
sign affixed above his head: JESUS OF NAZARETH, THE KING OF THE
JEWS. One half seemed to cancel out the other; the "Nazareth" part of the sign

made the "king" part look ridiculous. It was like saying he was from the projects, or from Soweto or the favelos of Rio. They were comrades now, having walked toward death together. The beloved disciple, hearing the criminal use this name, must have cringed at the familiarity.

Pray this, Jesus had said, "Your kingdom come. . . . " Had they ever done so? Often the gathered church prays the perfect prayer now, but had the disciples ever gathered together and prayed it in unison? Had Jesus ever said, "Okay, say it now; I want to be sure you know every word"? Had they thought much about what it was they were praying for? Surely in their most fevered dreams they had never suspected that the coming of the kingdom would involve events so gruesome and horrible.

The horror of Calvary was a temporary camouflage that hid from ordinary eyes the coming of the kingdom of heaven. The very sign hanging askew over God's suffering servant, meant to mock Jesus and his people, was an unwitting proclamation of a truth so profound that the eventual restoration of all creation would flow from it. The dying thief read the sign and believed. The Holy Spirit was there, not only sustaining Jesus in his extremity and keeping him from being pulverized by God's wrath against our sin but also working in the heart of a wretched man.

He realized what we must also realize: two kingdoms clashed at Calvary's cross. One of them would inevitably plunge all who served it into the depths of hell; the other would raise its obedient subjects to paradise. In this man's plaintive call to Jesus, we see what faith must be, even now, for us.

Our faith is in Jesus of Nazareth, God in humbled flesh. Our faith, like that of the thief on the cross, must believe that Jesus of Nazareth conquered death not only for himself but also for all those who trust in him. Our faith must realize that Jesus' kingdom is coming even when everything seems in place to destroy it. And our faith must understand that the kingdom will be established finally in the future.

As long as we are in this world, we pray for the coming of Christ's kingdom in a place filled with the venom of Christ-hating humanity. It seems absurd to pray like this here, where there seems to be no hope that the man from Nazareth will prevail.

But he surely will. The heavenly kingdom will be established. So we follow the thief into paradise, with his pathetic cry coming from deep within our hearts.

Jesus, remember me when you come into your kingdom. I am no better than the wretched thief. Give me hope as I try to follow you, my King and my God. Keep me from becoming discouraged by the other kingdom that seems to be victorious. May your kingdom come. Amen.

TWENTY-ONE

Hitting Delete

"Your will be done on earth as it is in heaven."
—Matthew 6:10

Anyone who uses a computer knows that every once in a while you can lose everything because somehow, inadvertently, you hit the delete key. And sometimes when you're trying to save a file, you do it wrong and it disappears forever. It can make a grown man weep.

We don't often think about it, but there's also a "delete key" in the Lord's Prayer. Usually we override it so it doesn't do us much harm when we hit it.

When we pray that God's will be done on earth as it is in heaven, we are actually asking God to delete our own will so that we can become like the angels who do God's will without a question.

The reference to heaven in the perfect prayer reminds us that there is a realm where the will of God is absolutely supreme. That's where the angels are: "Praise the LORD, you his angels, you mighty ones who do his bidding, who obey his word" (Ps. 103:20).

When we pray the perfect prayer, we are praying for our world also to be populated by those who do God's bidding. And the logical place for such obedience to start is within ourselves.

Those who want to live eternal life beginning now realize that God's will must be supreme. Therefore, it is appropriate for us to ask God to delete our own will and substitute God's will. The best way for this to happen is for our will to become like God's will. And that happens when we live close to God and earnestly, regularly, practice the spiritual disciplines the Bible reveals.

Exhibit number one of a person who obeyed God as the angels do is Joseph's wife, Mary. Gabriel, a really top angel, stood before her one day, greeted her respectfully, and told her she was going to have a baby. Responding to her puzzlement, Gabriel explained how it was going to happen. He told her that the child who would be born would be called "the Son of God." Mary responded to the obedient angel with her own obedience: "I am the Lord's servant. May it be to me as you have said" (Luke 1:38).

"I am the Lord's servant." That's really what we are saying when we pray that God's will be done on earth as it is in heaven. When we think about the Lord's Prayer this way, it almost seems as if Jesus tricked us into asking for something that we really don't want. Yes, we would like to serve God to some significant degree, but serving him like the angels do—with God's will supreme and ours deleted—is not exactly what we have in mind.

That we are not more enthusiastic about this is a symptom of our great religious problem. We are too easily satisfied with the level of spiritual life that we have. Churches can actually be a deterrent to our becoming the followers of Christ that God wants us to be. Churches can provide us with standards that give us the impression that we are okay. Go to church a prescribed number of times, give a certain amount of money, support good causes, maybe teach church school and be a deacon or a preacher—check 'em off and you can see that you are a pretty good Christian. You are at least as good as a lot of people and a lot better than many.

But Jesus tells us that we should ask God to give us a transplant, like a kidney transplant. Take out my will, we should pray, and replace it with God's will. God wants us to be like an angel. But thank you, Lord, we really prefer not to be like angels . . . yet. There's plenty of time for that later. Meanwhile, we've got a lot to do—moving ahead in our careers, shopping for the things we want, doing what most everyone else does.

The trouble with God's will being done on earth—that is, in my life—is that then I am going to be more like God, and I'm not quite ready for that. Exactly. "Be imitators of God, therefore, as dearly loved children and live a life of love, just as Christ loved us and gave himself up for us as a fragrant offering and sacrifice to God" (Eph. 5:1).

God wants us to be more and more like him. Remember, that's the way God created us—in his image. And God wants that image restored in us. Even Jesus had to pray to his Father, "Not my will but yours be done." Jesus did God's will on earth perfectly, and we must ask for grace to be like him.

Father in heaven, it's so very hard for us to put our own will aside and submit to yours. It's so hard. May we truly believe that this is what you want from us. And please give us this holy transplant. For Jesus' sake, Amen.

TWENTY-TWO

The Bread of Heaven

"Give us today our daily bread."
—Matthew 6:11

Most elements in the Lord's Prayer have an eternal reference. But in the middle of the prayer is this reference to the bread we need each day. Does this have an eternal reference too?

In this prayer, Jesus uses our daily bread as a representative of all of the material necessities we need. Bread stands for all our food, our clothing, and our shelter. Will we have need of any of these in glory? Will we need bread?

In 1 Corinthians 6:13 the apostle Paul seems to indicate that we will not do any eating when we are glorified: He writes, "'Food for the stomach and the stomach for food'—but God will destroy them both." This simple enough statement seems to tell us that there will be no food in heaven and no digestive systems to process food.

Several other passages in the Bible, however, require us to be careful with this conclusion. For one thing, we know that Jesus ate with his disciples after his resurrection. If we believe in the resurrection of the body, as the Apostles' Creed puts it, there is reason to think that the very same body that we put in the grave will be raised again.

When Jesus rose from the grave, he said to his disciples: "'Look at my hands and my feet. It is myself! Touch me and see; a ghost does not have flesh and bones, as you see I have'" (Luke 24:39). The passage continues: "When he had said this, he showed them his hands and feet. And while they still did not believe it because of joy and amazement, he asked them, 'Do you have anything here to eat?' They gave him a piece of broiled fish, and he took it and ate it in their presence" (vv. 40-43).

This is a remarkable vignette. When this same Jesus ascended into heaven, the disciples were told that he was going to return as they had seen him leave. So there is every reason to believe that the body Jesus has in heaven at this very moment is the same body he had when he appeared to his disciples. And Jesus ate with his resurrected body.

Jesus also talked with his disciples about drinking with them in glory. Matthew, Mark, and Luke all record Jesus saying, when he established the sacrament of the Lord's Supper, that he would not drink of the cup again with his disciples until he drank with them in his coming kingdom.

In addition, Revelation 2:7 tells us that those who overcome will eat of the tree of life that is in the paradise of God.

It is interesting that bread is the only reference to our physical needs in the Lord's Prayer, and bread, of course, is something we eat. While it is true that physical food will ultimately be destroyed and our stomachs will be destroyed as well, apparently there will be something in heaven that will correspond to the sustenance and the pleasure that we derive from eating.

Eating is not only a necessity but is a great physical pleasure as well. Think of Esau—a ravenous man who was willing to give up what was most precious to him so that he could have his lentil stew. We have all known such hunger, possibly after a round of strenuous exercise. We know the grand experience of enjoying a feast with our dear friends. All the rich viands, each with its delicious flavor, provide an overpowering delight.

How God will accomplish this in the new order that he has for us, none of us can tell. But Jesus told his disciples that he was looking forward to a blessed meal with them in the eternal kingdom.

"Give us this day our daily bread." We humbly implore God for it today, and as we do, we know that the day will come when this prayer will be answered in a manner that will fill us with eternal delight. When the kingdom fully comes and when the will of God is supreme throughout the universe, we will feast with Christ in glory. How God will accomplish this, we have no idea; but we know that it will surely happen.

Creator God, we are eager to see how you will establish the new earth where righteousness will dwell, and where we will dwell with bodies like Jesus' body. We are eager for the eternal pleasures you have for your people. In Christ's name, Amen.

TWENTY-THREE

No, Not Again!

"Forgive us our debts. . . . "
—Matthew 6:12

Why this torture?

Why do we have to ask God for forgiveness every day? Thinking about our sin, after all, is not very pleasant. Is it psychologically healthy every single day to remember that I am a sinner?

And another thing: what kind of a God is it who requires us to keep coming to him this way? Isn't there a "once for all" side to this forgiveness business? In fact, Hebrews 9:26 tells us that Jesus appeared once for all at the end of the ages to do away with sin. It's all supposed to be taken care of: "Believe in the Lord Jesus, and you will be saved" (Acts 16:31). I believe in Christ, so why must I ask God for forgiveness every single day?

We ask questions like these because we don't really understand the debt we owe God. Jesus knew all about Hebrews 9:26 when he instructed his disciples to ask for forgiveness every day. He knew that within months, he would pay the full price for all that debt, every last denarius. But he also knew that having a proper relationship with his heavenly Father requires that we never fail to ask him for forgiveness. Never.

Not even in heaven? Most likely not in the same way, but even there, we will not for one moment forget our sins. Every time we see Jesus, we will see him as the Lamb of God who takes away the sin of the world. The Lion of the tribe of Judah will always appear as the Lamb who has been slain (Rev. 5:5-6). We'll be a lot smarter then, and whenever we see him we will remember why he had to be slain: because of our sin.

Our biggest sin is that we continually trivialize sin. We know it's wrong to do this or that, to think this or that—but come on, we tell ourselves, let's not make a mountain out of a molehill. I wonder what was going through Adam's mind when God came looking for him. To be sure, he was scared and tried to hide, but could he, even then, have thought somehow that God would at least give him another chance? Did he really understand that he had committed an act that affected the universe? One thing is sure: Adam's children have never considered sin terribly serious.

Sin is a trillion times more serious than we imagine, and so we must ask for forgiveness every day. And we must ask because the forgiveness of our sins, though made possible once for all at Calvary, becomes a reality each day as we engage in confession and contrition and repentance. Granted, we can easily convince ourselves that it is not really necessary to ask yet again that our sins be forgiven. But God, who is the expert on this subject, knows that our sin grows with each daily addition. Each day anew, we must confess that we have sinned again and we must ask our Father to remove from our record what we have again added to it by our sin.

We would much prefer, though, to make our peace with God once for all and then forget about asking for forgiveness any further. But our preference is not the decisive factor. God's will is decisive, and God wants us to ask for forgiveness repeatedly.

Jesus once told a parable that established the necessity for confession of sin. Two men went into the temple to pray, one of them a self-righteous religious type who praised God because he was better than anyone he had met so far. The other fellow crouched next to the exit, pounding on his chest with clenched fists, and, eyes downcast, asked God for mercy. It was the mercy-asker who went home justified, Jesus said.

The apostle Paul, who knew that grace was amazing and free and totally effective because it had saved him, a persecutor of the church, cried out to God for forgiveness. At the end of his life, Christ's crusty soldier called himself the chief of sinners. In Romans 7 he describes the terrible fight that went on inside him every day as he tried to live for Christ, struggling daily against the old nature that kept him from doing so 100 percent.

We may not like the simple fact that Christianity is for sinners. Only for sinners. Anyone who feels that today, at least, he or she has made it through without adding to the vile debt of sin against the perfect God, has yet to learn what Christianity is all about. It's about poor sinners daily asking for forgiveness. And receiving it.

Heavenly Father, forgive me once again for thinking that I don't have to keep asking for your forgiveness. You know my sin perfectly; I only know it partially. Please forgive me in this day. For Jesus' sake, Amen.

TWENTY-FOUR

Our Cry for Help

"And lead us not into temptation, but deliver us from the evil one."
—Matthew 6:13

We always say the Lord's Prayer wrong. Why? Because we always end it with a statement that Jesus didn't end it with. "For thine is the kingdom and the power and the glory forever, Amen" is not a bad thing to say, but Jesus didn't end the prayer that way. Instead he ended it with an ear-splitting cry for help.

We end it with a doxology and that's okay, but it obscures what Jesus had in mind when he ended it with a call for proper steering and deliverance. Steer us in the right direction so that we avoid those places where temptation is so strong we won't have a chance of standing up to it. And deliver us from evil.

If we could see what Jesus could see, we would stop saying the Lord's Prayer like third-graders reciting a nice poem. When Jesus taught his followers to pray, he concluded with a petition that reflected what he saw. What he saw in the hearts of human beings made him sad and angry. He saw manifestations of evil in the deformation of true religion that had taken place among the Jewish people. He saw the horrible threat of demonic hosts who would rest at nothing in order to destroy his work. Because he could see all this with perfect clarity, he concluded the perfect prayer the way he did.

Nobody calls for help in the tone of voice we usually use when we conclude the Lord's Prayer. By the time we get to that part, we are winding down, and once we finish it, we swing into the beautiful doxology that we have added to the prayer as if we are singing a hymn.

I shall never forget my experience of drowning several decades ago. (The memory is still very vivid to me.) I went down once and bobbed to the surface; I went down again and bobbed to the surface; I went down the third time and stayed down. But someone came out from shore and rescued me. Why? Because the two times I broke the surface, I called for help as loudly as I could. When my wife heard my cry, she knew I was terrified.

That is really the way the Lord Jesus designed the Lord's Prayer—it is supposed to end with a call for help. That call for help is supposed to *sound* like a call for help. Nobody ever calls for help in an emergency by saying quietly, "If it's convenient, would you please come over here and rescue me." No, when injury and death are staring us in the face, we shout out as loudly as we can, pleading for rescue.

When Jesus sees his people, bound for eternity but still in this world, he sees vulnerable creatures who pray, yes, but who are nonetheless in serious danger. Not only are we surrounded by all sorts of temptations and threats outside ourselves, but threats to our spiritual well-being also exist within ourselves. In fact, as soon as the Lord's Prayer is concluded, within seconds after we have asked for forgiveness of sins, Jesus speaks to us about the fact that we must forgive others. In other words, Jesus realizes that it is very possible for people like us, who ask for forgiveness, to miss the point of forgiving grace entirely and to become vindictive. Jesus knows the tendencies within our cursed hearts. He knows the temptations within and without. So when you finish praying, he says, always ask God to deliver you from the sin all around you and the sin within you.

Obviously, after all these years of praying the Lord's Prayer as we have, there will be no changing of it so that it stops where Jesus ended it. There will be no changing our way of saying it so that when we stop there, we will call out, "Deliver us from evil!" with the plaintive cry of a drowning man. No, we will not be able to change those things. But perhaps now that we have thought about this, we will say the prayer differently in our hearts and in our lives.

When we see the threat on every side, we need to be a little frantic. And then we need to cry for help the way frantic people do.

O Lord Jesus Christ, teach us to pray the way you want us to pray. Show us the sin around us and the sin within. And enable us to pray for the deliverance that we need so desperately. Respond to our cry for help with your salvation. Amen.

TWENTY-FIVE

Praying in the Spirit

Pray in the Spirit on all occasions with all kinds of prayers and requests.
—Ephesians 6:18

P rayer is such a mystery! Often when we start talking about it, all sorts of questions come up that leave us looking at one another in puzzlement. We sometimes wonder whether prayer makes any sense at all. Fortunately, we don't stop praying.

We all know some of the questions. Why pray if God knows our needs before we start? Why pray if God knows what he is going to do already before we pray? And why pray when we have experiences that make us feel that God is as deaf as a stone—God's just not listening (too busy maybe)? And then there's the missionary question: If God knows who will be saved, why do I have to pray for the salvation of the folks next door or those who keep resisting the gospel in Katmandu?

Questions like these are bound to come up whenever we take our small minds and start thinking about the very idea of talking with God. With God, mind you, the Creator of all, the controller of every event that happens in this world—not just flights of Air Force One but also the events we can observe only through an electron microscope. We come to this God with our prayers. It really doesn't make any sense at all, does it?

Prayer does not make any "sense" in the usual sense because it is not a usual human activity. That is, it is not a human activity like, let's say, figuring out the sum of 26 and 83. Or like painting a house. Prayer is something human beings cannot do unless they are dressed and filled by God.

Ephesians 6 describes the uniform of prayer: a special belt, breastplate, sandals, shield, helmet, and sword. The belt is God's truth, the breastplate is righteousness, the sandals are gospel Birkenstocks, the helmet is salvation itself, the shield is unbreakable faith, and the sword is the power of the Spirit of God. When believers are fully outfitted this way, what they do cannot be fully understood.

Then, in Ephesians 6:18, we learn that this elaborate gear is all designed to make Christians pray-ers: "And pray in the Spirit on all occasions with all kinds of prayers and requests. With this in mind be alert and always keep on praying for all the saints."

What we have here is God on the outside and God on the inside. Believers pray "in the Spirit." It is the Holy Spirit who inclines our hearts to pray. It is the Holy Spirit who supplies us with the determination to make sure there's time every day to pray. And it is the Holy Spirit who accompanies our prayers, even molds and edits them as he prepares them for divine consideration. This is not some dream I'm dreaming here. This is the way the Bible describes prayer. Surely it is all implied in the idea "pray *in the Spirit.*"

We are talking here about the spiritual person, and by "spiritual person" we mean one who has been transformed by the Spirit of God into God's child; one who has become the dwelling place of God in the Spirit. When such people pray, they draw their resources for their intercessions from the Holy Spirit within them.

The apostle Paul spells out for us what this means in Romans 8. "You received the Spirit of sonship. And by him we cry, *'Abba,* Father.' The Spirit himself testifies with our spirit that we are God's children" (vv. 15-16). He goes on to explain, "The Spirit helps us in our weakness. We do not know what we ought to pray for, but the Spirit himself intercedes for us with groans that words cannot express. And he who searches our hearts knows the mind of the Spirit, because the Spirit intercedes for the saints in accordance with God's will" (vv. 26-27).

Prayer is a spiritual activity. Once we realize that we pray dressed in clothing God provides and energized by God's very presence within us, all the questions we raise become pointless. Remember the questions at the beginning? If we think of prayer as simply a human activity, it may seem senseless. But when we understand that prayer is something we do when we are transformed by God and filled with God, those questions become senseless.

Prayer is the most excellent activity we engage in while we are in this world. It prepares us for forever by giving us a taste of forever today.

Loving God, you know that sometimes our minds can run away with us and we can begin to feel that prayer is futile. Spirit of the living God, clothe us with the armor of grace and fill us so that the prayers we bring will be wonderfully effective. For Jesus' sake, Amen.

TWENTY-SIX

Wanting His Wants

If we ask anything according to his will, he hears us.
—1 John 5:14

One of the amazing things about believing in Christ and knowing that we are eternal is the experience of answered prayer. To pray to God for specific things and to see them realized over time fills us with a unique emotion. There are no words for it. It feels something like pride, yet it is pride's opposite because it glories in the power of God. Just to think that we could be part of God's great action in the world or in someone's life is overwhelming.

When believers think of themselves as those who have been rescued from destruction, those who are filled with God's Spirit and are already experiencing eternal life, it is not surprising that they participate in God's work in the world through their prayers. Actually, it is surprising because, after all, we are very small and insignificant in ourselves. So we must take into account the Bible's repeated message that prayer must be continuous and that prayer is effective.

John refers several times in his gospel and in his general epistles to the surety of answered prayer spoken in the name of Christ, and, in 1 John 5, when it is congruent with his will. Remember that this apostle wrote as he did after years of firsthand knowledge of the surety of God's answer to believers' prayers. He was no novice.

"This is the confidence we have in approaching God," says John, "that if we ask anything according to his will, he hears us. And if we know that he hears us—whatever we ask—we know that we have what we asked of him" (1 John 5:14-15). This is an extremely strong statement; it borders on the presumptuous. The word *confidence* is, in the original, the trademark word for the demeanor of believers who are full of the Spirit of God and feel themselves buoyed up by divine power. It's the word used of Peter and John when they were brought before the court that had sent Christ to the cross: "When they saw the *courage* of Peter and John . . . " It's the word used of the way Paul preached the gospel—boldness. And the word for *ask* is strong as well.

We sense, however, that the key to receiving what we ask for is that what we ask for must be according to the will of God. That's the catch. Improperly understood, it can cause cynicism. Surely if I ask God for what he was going to give anyway or for what he was going to do anyway, what I ask for will come to pass. But if that's the case, it's something like the lottery: hit the right number and you'll win. How can we know the will of God?

If this statement stood alone, outside the rest of the message of the Bible, we would become cynics for sure. But those who know the Bible's entire message know that God isn't playing a game with us here. Think of this statement, for example, in connection with the great promises of the Holy Spirit, who puts believers on God's wavelength so that they begin to think the way God thinks. We must remember that this promise is given to a very special kind of people, people who have been "born of God," an idea found in this same chapter. They are people of faith: "This is the victory that overcomes the world, even our faith. Who is it that overcomes the world? Only he who believes that Jesus is the Son of God" (1 John 5:4-5).

These are people who have been purged of the usual avarice and selfishness. They are not keeping prayer journal notes on when they asked for prosperity and made a mint on Microsoft. They are part of God's people, the church, immersed in God's holy Word, disciplined in obedience to the Lord. They discuss the will of God with like-minded men and women. And they pray for magnificent things like the increasing revelation of Christ's kingdom and the continuing glory of his name and reputation among us. The magnificent subjects of their prayers involve specific events that are part of all this, including prayers for healing and for conversion and even for daily bread. In fact, God's people ask for great things—things like the tearing down of the Berlin Wall, the destruction of Communism, and a great regeneration of life on the North American continent as more and more people turn to the Savior.

God inspires such prayers, and God delights in answering them.

O God, inhabit our lives with your presence and mold us with your power, that we will sense your will as we bring our daily requests. Inspire us with the confidence that accompanies the certainty of knowing that we are praying according to your will. We pray in Jesus' name. Amen.

TWENTY-SEVEN

Praying for Each Other

"I pray . . . that you may be filled to the measure of all the fullness of God."
—Ephesians 3:16, 19

"Please heal Rosie of her urinary tract infection." "Please make Tim stop living with that awful girl—show him the error of his ways." "Bring a lot of neighborhood kids to our Bible school." "And be with Bill and Amanda and their children as they work in Uganda." So we pray.

Let's continue to pray this way, but let's pray for more . . . the way Ephesians 3 shows us. Whenever I read that chapter I realize how often my prayers fall short of what they ought to include for people I love. I must pray that they will be "filled to the measure of the fullness of God." Everything else is secondary.

Why don't I pray for what Ephesians 3:14-20 describes? I suspect it's because I don't long for what this passage talks about for myself. I pray for secondary things for myself, and that's why I pray for secondary things for others too.

Ephesians is full of prayers. Chapter 3, verses 14-20, tell us what the apostle Paul prayed for when he was on his knees before the Father, "from whom his whole family in heaven and on earth derives its name." He prayed for something none of us would dare suggest might be a possibility for anybody: that they would be filled "to the measure of all the fullness of God."

We must be careful with an idea like this. Is there something here that can help us figure out what this might possibly mean?

First of all, we must understand that this has everything to do with what's inside a person. Paul wants God to strengthen the Ephesians "with power through his Spirit" in their "inner being." From this we can draw a simple conclusion: no one can be a Christian without being changed inside. We have to be converted. Being a

Christian is not about taking on a Christian lifestyle and fitting into a Christian community. It's what's inside that counts, what's in the heart. We have to pray for inner transformation for ourselves and for others.

Specifically, the apostle prayed that Christ would "dwell in your hearts through faith." But Christ is in heaven. So what does this mean? It means that Christ, whose flesh is in heaven, has sent the promised Holy Spirit into the world where he lives within believers. We cannot have faith unless the Holy Spirit activates that faith within us, and when we have faith, Christ becomes the center of our attention.

Believing parents whose hearts are broken because of the behavior of a child who has heard of Christ at the family table, who has gone to church and possibly even been educated in Christian schools, and who now is living a godless life, need to get down on their knees before the Father and plead with him to send Christ into their child's heart. "O Jesus Christ, move into Bill's heart and take over, that's all I ask." They have to pray that on Tuesday, and then again on Wednesday, and Friday—all week long, every week. Only Christ in Bill's heart is going to help. Nothing else will.

"Filled to the measure of all the fullness of God" means that believers, filled with the presence of Christ through the Holy Spirit, will be overwhelmed by the wonder of God's love. How can you tell if a person is full of Christ? Do you tell by asking if they know all sorts of Bible trivia? By asking if they know theology and doctrine? By noting their position in the church? None of these make them full of Christ. You can know church doctrine, you can even know the Bible very well and not have Christ inside you.

People who have Christ in their hearts are people whose main thought is about the love of Christ. The God-given power they have enables them to think of Christ's love, even to grasp how wide and how long and how high and how deep it is. They know "the love that surpasses knowledge."

People like this stagger through life, in a sense, overwhelmed by what God has done for them in Jesus Christ. The cross, where divine love was poured out in Christ's unblemished blood, is the center of their attention. People whose hearts are overcome with their contemplation of this marvelous love are filled "to the measure of all the fullness of God."

Blessed Father, my main prayer for those I love is that they will be filled with your presence, changed within, overwhelmed with their knowledge of your love for them. I want this for myself too.
Come, Lord Jesus, and fill our poor, poor hearts. Amen.

TWENTY-EIGHT

The Forever Sign

*[You were] buried with him in baptism and raised
with him through your faith in the power of God.*
—Colossians 2:12

There is a sign that identifies the people who belong to God now and forever. It is a watermark, and just as you have to hold one of our new twenties up to the light before you can see Jackson's watermarked picture, so God holds us up to the light of Christ and sees the mark of his blood on us as plain as day.

Satan's host also see this sign. Whenever they come upon a person with the watermark of Christ's blood, they know that God has been there first.

For Christians who view baptism as the New Testament covenant sign that takes the place of the Old Testament sign of circumcision, it is clear that baptism is a household event that flows from God's claim upon believers and their children. Colossians 2 sets up the equation for us: Circumcision in the Old Testament gives way to baptism in the new. New Testament believers were circumcised "with a circumcision not done by the hands of men, but . . . by Christ" (v. 11). Baptism is the fulfillment of circumcision in several ways.

For one thing, baptism is a covenant sign that is shared by men and women, by boy babies and girl babies. Second, it is deeper and more powerful. Circumcision was external; baptism, though applied externally, signifies a power that soaks into us and changes us within. To be sure, the Old Testament calls people to circumcise their hearts as well as their bodies, but that full reality could be realized only when Christ came and sent his Holy Spirit, who came to live within us.

Some believe that we should administer baptism only to those who have confessed their faith. To be sure, if a person has not been baptized before, she should receive the sacrament only when she believes in Christ as Savior. But even then, baptism should not be viewed as a sign of faith; rather, it is a sign of God's covenant mercies. It is the sign and seal of God's electing grace and irresistible love. That is as true of adult baptism as it is of the baptism of children of believers. Baptism is always a sign of God's action, not of human action. We are saved by God's action, not by ours.

It is exciting to see the way God has worked through the centuries, graciously enlarging the circle of those who are embraced within his covenant love. It comes as a startling surprise to learn that the Passover meal was made available to other than Israelites: "An alien living among you who wants to celebrate the LORD's Passover must have all the males in his household circumcised; then he may take part like one born in the land" (Ex. 12:48).

The covenant sign in the Old Testament announced that God would be the God of all those who would respond obediently to his love; those who departed from God's law were punished accordingly. So too, baptism today is no guarantee that the person baptized will automatically be saved. Baptism is the great reminder that the person baptized is in a special relationship with God and has enormous obligations to live obediently to the gospel.

The New Testament contains no command to adjust the administration of the covenant sign to exclude children. The opposite is the case: on several significant occasions those invited to believe in Jesus are told that their children also would benefit from their decision (Acts 2:39; 16:31).

The blessed sign of baptism impresses us with the way God sweeps into our lives with matchless grace. Now we must respond. But not even our response is energized by our own will and power; it is a gift of God. So we seek to live obediently, especially in our marriages and homes where we teach our children God's way. We passionately guard our homes against intrusion by evil powers and live as joyful members of the covenant community—Christ's holy church.

Baptism has eternal significance. In the book of Revelation, the angel cries out, "Do not harm the land or the sea or the trees until we put a seal on the foreheads of the servants of our God" (Rev. 7:3). Once the water of the sacrament evaporates, it's gone; but God sees it forever.

The truth is that baptism is the most important event of our life. There is nothing greater than the day God reaches down and signs us with the blood of his Son and declares, "You are mine."

Father of Jesus Christ, who shed his blood so that his holy sign could be placed on your people, we praise you for the grace of the blessed sacrament of baptism. May those of us who have received the sign remember it always and live accordingly. Amen.

TWENTY-NINE

Remaining in Christ

See that what you have heard from the beginning remains in you.
If it does, you also will remain in the Son. . . .
—1 John 2:24

O nce we realize that the Bible teaches that salvation is by grace alone, "not by works, so that no one can boast" (Eph. 2:9), we must also believe in what is sometimes called "the perseverance of the saints." If God saves people—they do not save themselves—it is inconceivable that God would save them for a time and then let them drop back into their former condition. As the apostle Paul told the Philippians, "[I am confident] that he who began a good work in you will carry it on to completion until the day of Christ Jesus" (Phil. 1:6).

Actually, the so-called perseverance of the saints is the perseverance of God. Some believers I know don't like this teaching because they say that it makes people careless. I agree: it *can* make people careless. Some who believe that once they are saved, they can never become unsaved, use this teaching to justify their disinterest in the things of Christ and his church. They attend worship services; they go through the motions; but they figure that their salvation is like having a certificate of deposit in the bank—it will be there for them when they need it.

This is scary. The same Bible that teaches that God will bring his people through to glory also indicates that we have to be very careful each day that we do not lose what we have. Does that seem like a contradiction? It is. But it is a reality that we find throughout the Bible.

For example, when Christ was born in Bethlehem, it was absolutely certain and sure that he would be obedient unto death and would rise victorious. Nevertheless, he had to walk each step between Bethlehem and Golgotha; he couldn't helicopter over the top of it all. He had to experience each day. Along the way, he was severely tempted. He wept. He cried out in anguish. His struggle was real. And those whom the devil will never snatch from the Father's hand must struggle too.

So the Bible uses language that describes our daily lives as precarious. First John 2:18-27 is such a passage. Here believers are reminded of their "anointing from the Holy One" which enables them to know the truth and reject error. These believers were told the truth about the Lord Jesus Christ—that he was a real human being and that he was the Son of God.

But over the years, as always happens, some infiltrated the ranks of the church and raised doubts about the true humanity of Christ and about his true divinity. So the apostle John wrote to warn the believers. He said, "I am writing these things to you about those who are trying to lead you astray." He did not assume that these people were simply the elect of God and false teaching would slide off them like water off a duck's back. He viewed them as people involved in a real struggle. He appealed to their anointing, the presence of the Holy Spirit in their lives that had enabled them to receive the truth about Christ Jesus. As they were being tempted to believe teachings that contradicted what they had learned, the apostle encouraged them to remain in the truth they had received.

"See that what you have heard from the beginning remains in you. If it does, you also will remain in the Son and in the Father. And this is what he promised us— even eternal life." The key word in this section is "remain." Remaining in the truth that brings salvation requires steadfast determination. This command is spoken to all of us as believers.

One of the ways God guarantees that those who are saved will remain in the kingdom is by coming to us and commanding us to resist evil and falsehood and remain in the truths we have received.

The teaching that those who are saved by grace will be saved to the end has its dangerous side. If we think this means that our salvation is cut and dried, we are dead wrong. Believers' lives involve the earnest application of mind and heart to knowing the truth and resisting evil. Just as Christ's temptations were real, so are ours.

Thankfully, we have received an anointing from the Holy One. "But as his anointing teaches you about all things and as that anointing is real, not counterfeit—just as he has taught you, remain in him" (v. 27). That's an imperative.

Thank you, O Father, for anointing us with the Spirit of Christ.
Help us use what we have received through our anointing to
discern truth and falsehood. Help us resist the powerful forces
that seek to turn us away from Christ. In his name, Amen.

THIRTY

The Mystical Union

"On that day you will realize that I am in my Father,
and you are in me, and I am in you."
—John 14:20

I come from a tradition that seldom talks about the mystical union. It is noted in seminary theology classes, but for the most part this teaching could well be a recipe tucked away in a yellowed cookbook.

No wonder people like me are so weak and ineffective. The Bible clearly tells us that when we believe in Jesus, he moves into our house, and he takes his Father with him. Jesus said, "If anyone loves me, he will obey my teaching. My Father will love him, and we will come to him and make our home with him" (John 14:23).

Verse 20 is even more striking. Looking forward to his resurrection, Jesus said, "On that day you will realize that I am in my Father, and you are in me, and I am in you."

I saw this statement highlighted for the first time at a funeral twenty or so years ago by Dr. Alexander C. De Jong. He invited us to visualize envelopes. Jesus is in God the Father and believers are in Jesus. But the end of the sentence baffles us: we are envelopes too, and Jesus is in us. Like everything else that's truly biblical, the truth defies logic and visualization. Finally we are left with this single powerful point: *Believers are united with God the Father through Jesus Christ, who is united with them.*

Yes, *mystical* union is a good name for this truth: the mystery defies our minds as we try to comprehend it. It is also mystical in the sense that it is a reality that does not depend on the usual spatial and material categories we work with; it is a spiritual reality, untouchable and unfathomable.

It's impossible to conceptualize this. But we don't have to do that either. What is important is that we believe that the mystical union is real, and that we determine to live in the power of God, who is within us.

Surely, these realities are what make us eternal people. Christians do not persevere in their faith because they have a bulldog determination to hang on to the bitter end. When the apostle Paul told the Philippian Christians that he was confident that God who had begun a good work in them would carry it through to completion (1:6), his confidence was rooted in the power of God, not in the faith record of the Philippians.

We believers make so many embarrassing mistakes simply because we ignore the resources available through our union with our Savior and his Father and the Holy Spirit. We are, in fact, united with the triune God. It took the Father, the Son, and the Holy Spirit, working together, to accomplish our salvation; and it takes the Father, the Son, and the Holy Spirit, working together, to keep us on track.

We often marvel when God uses us to accomplish events that leave us stunned. Sometimes we witness unusual answers to prayer, unusual achievements in ministry, unusual expressions of faithfulness to Christ in the workplace, in art, or in literature. And we wonder how God could use common people to accomplish these. Why are we surprised? If Christ died and rose again in order to equip us with the very presence of the Father, Son, and Holy Spirit, we should expect great things.

Forever people realize that their "foreverness" is what it is because they are united to the eternal God, who never deserts them. Whatever we must face—persecution, daunting challenge, mortal illness, financial ruin—God will be right there with us, closer than close. And whatever we face in terms of enormous challenge and opportunity, God will equip us to succeed.

Along with all the sins for which we ask forgiveness, we must also ask God to forgive us for not using our full potential—potential that exists because we are in Christ and Christ is in us and he is in the Father and the Father is in us. Possibly this should be our first and foremost call for forgiveness, because our failure to live out of God's power has compromised our effectiveness.

There is really no limit to what God can accomplish in us and through us. "You, dear children, are from God and have overcome [the antichrist spirits], because the one who is in you is greater than the one who is in the world" (1 John 4:4).

Triune God, we repent of our sin of neglecting to live as people who are sustained and indwelt by the power of the Father, the Son, and the Holy Spirit. Use us to accomplish your goals in this day and all the days of our lives and forever. Amen.

THIRTY-ONE

How to Live Forever

*Whoever eats my flesh and drinks my blood has eternal life,
and I will raise him up at the last day.*
—John 6:54

The bad news is that normal human cells have a limited capacity to proliferate. Eventually time runs out—cells age and stop dividing. The time remaining in a cell's life depends on the length of the telomeres—repeated sequences of DNA on the ends of chromosomes that protect the tips from degradation. Research shows that human cells grow older because each time they divide their telomeres shorten.

The good news is that scientists have discovered that by introducing the enzyme telomerase into human cells, their life spans can be prolonged. In our pampered and wealthy culture this is bound to cause excitement. Can't you just hear people say, "Pass me some of that telomerase, will you?"

Those who think in biblical terms know that this is baloney. True, cells in a dish do very well when telomerase is stirred into the mixture, but that has little to do with what actually goes on in our complicated bodies. To be sure, some alternative medicine Internet site will soon be offering such a substance with the gleeful promise that it will help us live to 150. But in reality, no one who reads this is going to benefit from ideas that promise to double the human life span.

Human beings may tinker with their little cells all they want, but the fact is that innumerable factors limit human life, not the least of which is the sheer diminishing of the desire to live when our friends and family have already left the scene. But let there be no mistake: Christianity is about extending our life span—for eternity. That means *forever*. And when we read John 6, we learn that this extension actually does have something to do with our bodies.

This chapter reports Jesus' miraculous feeding of as many as 6,000 people; he used five loaves and two fish to do it. The chapter also tells us about comments Jesus made, possibly the very next day, when he was home in Capernaum. His comments then were about food, but, to the shock of everyone who heard him, he talked about his own body as food—his flesh and his blood. You have to eat it, he said, if you want eternal life. None of this telomerase, just Jesus; you have to eat his flesh and drink his blood.

Jesus is using sacramental language here, language that he explained later when, after celebrating the Jewish Passover with his disciples, he introduced another meal that consisted of bread and wine. As he handed the bread to his disciples, he said, "Take and eat; this is my body." He did the same with the wine: "Drink from it, all of you. This is my blood . . . " (Matt. 26:26-28). In so doing, Jesus gave the church the sacrament of the Lord's Supper. Today, believers in Christ know that when they eat this holy supper in faith—*in faith*—they are united with the Lord Jesus Christ.

In the seventeenth century those who believed this and who were being persecuted, even killed for their faith, wrote the following about the Lord's Supper:

> To represent to us this spiritual and heavenly bread Christ has instituted an earthly and visible bread as the sacrament of his body and wine as the sacrament of his blood. He did this to testify to us that just as truly as we take and hold the sacraments in our hands and eat and drink it in our mouths, by which our life is then sustained, so truly we receive into our souls, for our spiritual life, the true body and true blood of Christ, our only Savior. We receive these by faith, which is the hand and mouth of our souls.
>
> —Belgic Confession, Article 35

Those who want to live forever need only believe in Jesus as the Son of God and their Savior. That is all. His declaration shocked his followers when they first heard it. It shocks us still. But it is unspeakably precious: "Whoever eats my flesh and drinks my blood has eternal life, and I will raise him up at the last day."

On second thought: you can keep the telomerase; we believers won't be needing it, thank you.

Lord Jesus Christ, we are overwhelmed with the wonder of what you have done for us. You have given us our faith, and through that faith you have united us with yourself—actually with your glorified body already while we are in this world. We praise you and adore you, our glorious Savior. Amen.

THIRTY-TWO

Win/Win

For to me to live is Christ and to die is gain.
—Philippians 1:21

Many who read this know the feeling: living from CT scan to CT scan, with a Gallium scan thrown in once in a while for good measure. Remission— it's a "whoopee" word. When you hear it the first time, it's like the sun coming up again after months of gloom. Lights go on all over the place. For a little while you don't have to think about dying. First it's every three months, and when you walk away and the doctor says everything looks okay, you feel wonderful. Then it's every six months. After a year or so, you begin to think, Maybe, just maybe, this cancer is really gone, really and truly. People begin to treat you normally once again. They don't keep asking: "How're ya doin?"

But you cannot escape anxiety. It keeps building up as you approach another appointment with your oncologist. And every time there's a little twitch you can't explain, or a little pain that you never had before, or even a good case of the flu, you cannot help wondering if your enemy has returned. You could kick yourself for being so uptight about this thing, but you can't help it.

The day before writing this, I talked with a woman who knows this routine well. She had just come away from her regularly scheduled CT scan and she was greatly relieved. She told me how happy she was and then added, "Of course, I was ready for anything. If it didn't turn out all right I would just have to go into treatment again." Yes, that's the way it goes. You go into it apprehensive, ready (you think) for bad news if it has to be.

How do forever people handle this? Like everybody else. You cannot argue with emotions. Even so, there is a plus factor for those of us who must ride this roller

70

coaster. Believers can say what everybody else says: "I am ready for whatever happens." But we can say even more: "Do you know what? For me to live is Christ, and to die is gain."

This is always true for all those who truly trust in Christ, and we can say it all the time. But it takes on special meaning when it's not our brother, not our sister, but ourselves who are standing in the need of prayer because we're sick with a killer sickness. God gives us special comfort—times when we realize with new clarity that we really are in a win/win situation. If we live, we live with and for Christ, and if we die, we will do the same with a greater intensity in glory.

There are times in our lives when the forward view seems to go on forever. There are other times when we look ahead and our gaze is halted at a barrier, a wall wide and high that obscures the future. We do not know what's beyond the wall; we don't know whether we will be able to get over it or around it. We try to make plans and find ourselves stuttering, stumbling. How can we plan for next summer's vacation when the wall is there? We wonder if we will see our son graduate from high school or our daughter get married.

When Paul wrote, "For me to live is Christ and to die is gain," he was an older man in prison for his faith. He realized that he could still do a lot for the church he loved, but he also knew that it was all up to the Savior to determine how long it was going to be. He was a person who lived to the hilt, but he also knew that there was another level of life just beyond this one when he would be in Christ's presence, serving him in new and even more glorious ways.

CT-scan people who love Jesus learn to say what Paul said. And we must all learn that, because we are mistaken if we think that the road ahead goes on forever. We need to learn to live with Christ here, depending on him, receiving our instructions from him, feeling ourselves strengthened by him. And we need to remind ourselves daily that the future will be exciting and fulfilling.

Followers of Christ who have to be checked again and again to see if a life-threatening illness has returned can know that, whatever happens, they are going to be winners. Sure, they'd like to receive good news next week, but more important than that is the good news they already have.

Lord Jesus, surround our lives this day with a sense of your presence. May we speak to you in prayer, wait upon you for strength, and follow your direction. Blessed Savior, we are looking forward to enjoying your presence forever. Amen.

THIRTY-THREE

Orphans Not

"I will not leave you as orphans; I will come to you."
—John 14:18

O rphans are among the most pitiable of people—little children without parents to care for them. Jesus selected this image to describe what was going to happen after he left his disciples, first to go to the cross and later to ascend into heaven.

We tend to discount this orphan language somewhat. After all, most of these men likely had at least one of their parents. Besides, they were all grown up and self-sufficient. But as Jesus thought of what was going to happen when he left them, he viewed them as potential orphans. It would be that bad.

Those who have read the Bible for many years and have listened to countless sermons find it hard to really see the extraordinary quality of the thirty-six months Jesus spent with his disciples. God in the flesh walked with these men. We know from reports in the gospels that from the beginning of Christ's ministry there was high religious excitement wherever he went. People were amazed, ecstatic even, as they observed his miracles and heard him teach, not as the scribes but with divine authority.

The disciples had seen incredible events. They could feel in their bones that something world-shaking was afoot. The Holy Spirit had enabled them to cast out demons and heal the sick. Now Jesus was about to leave them. And he realized that for the disciples, his leaving would be like what happens when a toddler loses both parents at the same time and is left to fend for itself.

Jesus knew it would be crushing for them to be bereft of his power and his teaching. Suddenly they would be thrown on their own resources. They would be like little children without a father or mother to care for them. And so he addressed the immeasurable threat that hung over them. Orphans you will not be, he assured them. Why not? Because Jesus would return to them.

It is important for all of us who follow Christ to understand what Jesus was saying here. He was not merely assuring the disciples that something would be present in their lives to give them a bit of comfort in their bereavement. The word that the original Scripture puts in Jesus' mouth here is the word *orphan,* used only in one other place in the New Testament. The disciples would become the very opposite of orphans. Christ Jesus would come back and be with them in a new way.

When we read the sentences that surround John 14:18, we see that Jesus was thinking about the coming of the Holy Spirit, who would dwell within the church and within believers' hearts. Though Jesus was fully aware that he was moving toward what would be the most horrible experience any human being has ever experienced—so horrible that his divinity alone enabled him to sustain it—he also realized that what he was going to go through would usher in an exciting new age for his followers.

We believers cannot think about the Holy Spirit enough. It is a profound pity that many assume that interest in the Holy Spirit is the province of charismatics. Praise God—all true believers are charismatics in the biblical sense. The disciples were not going to become orphans; they were to become the opposite of orphans: charismatics, people filled with the Holy Spirit. The Holy Spirit actualizes the presence of Christ among us. "The Lord is the Spirit, and where the Spirit of the Lord is, there is freedom" (2 Cor. 3:17)

I will come to you, said Jesus. "Surely, I am with you always, to the very end of the age" (Matt. 28:20). Eternal life begins right now for those who believe in Christ. The very point of his ministry, his life and his death, is that through it his people would become the opposite of orphans. The Greek word *orphanos* was used to translate the Hebrew word for *fatherless* in the Greek version of the Old Testament. Believers are not Fatherless, we are not Sonless, we are not Holy Spiritless. The Holy Spirit makes the presence of Christ real within us, and those who have the Son have the Father also.

If we are not orphans, why do we so often act like orphans? We are overwhelmed by self-pity and fear. We do not begin to use the provision Jesus has made for us. We must stop acting like orphans; we must act like those who have been filled with the very presence of our victorious Savior.

Lord Jesus, we remember that Isaiah said you would be called Everlasting Father. Surely you have a Father heart for us as you help us escape the fear and confines of our orphan state. Help us to live in the power of your Spirit in this day. Amen.

THIRTY-FOUR

Keeping in God's Love

Keep yourselves in God's love as you wait for the mercy of our Lord Jesus Christ to bring you to eternal life.
—Jude 21

Jesus' brother Jude was a very sensitive person, self-conscious even. When he greeted the church, he was reluctant to refer to his family relationship with Jesus; he only mentioned that he was the brother of Jesus' brother James. Where Jesus was concerned, Jude had become his brother's slave. He did what Jesus wanted him to do.

In this case, Jesus wanted Jude to address the deteriorating situation in the church. If Jude had had his way, he would have preferred to write a glowing letter to the church that talked about the Christian faith in general, a kind of doxology. But when a church is falling apart, you have to talk about its pressing problems.

It is almost embarrassing to see what was happening in the church Jude addressed. Self-styled leaders were corrupting the church with the most foul teachings; they were telling the people that, since they had been saved by grace alone, they were free to live immoral, licentious lives. It's an old Satanic trick: somehow get people into sexual immorality—use the doctrine of grace to do it if you have to.

False teachers are still up to the same tricks, and people in the church still fall for them. So Jesus' brother, who didn't want to be known as Jesus' brother, reacted by pointing them to "our Lord Jesus Christ." Keep yourselves in God's love as you wait for his mercy, he said. It is God's mercy ultimately that brings believers into eternal life, true, but they have the responsibility of keeping themselves in God's love.

The book of Jude, tantalizingly short (it would have been great to have heard more from him), concludes with a strong emphasis on the way people who know they are headed for glory should live. Being saved certainly does not allow believers to slip back into moral lethargy. Rather, once we believe in the Savior, we are required to work at keeping ourselves in God's love.

We might think that it is really God's responsibility—not ours—to keep us in his love. Well, we couldn't do it without God's Spirit within us, but here the Bible directs the command to us: "Keep yourselves in God's love. . . . "

What does this mean?

It means that we must arrange our lives so that we always remember what God has done for us in Jesus Christ. Christians are people who daily remember what God has done to show his love at the cross of Calvary. Christians remember the fullness of God's mercy and goodness; they begin their day by thinking of the cross and of what their lives have become because of it. We cannot keep ourselves in God's love unless we remember what that love has involved.

Keeping ourselves in the love of God also means that we live in the consciousness that God continues to love us daily. Even when we stagger through terrible difficulties, we must actively remind ourselves that God is still with us and that God is caring for us through it all. When we remember that the Son of God's love, Jesus, has died for us, we have no reason to doubt that his love continues to surround us.

In addition, keeping ourselves in the love of God means that we earnestly seek to honor God with our lives. Jude was terrifically upset with what was happening among those he addressed in the early church. They were living like lost souls in a Hemingway novel. Apparently the false teachers who were enticing the people into immoral lives had succeeded in convincing at least some of them to live like pigs. Jude was appalled. He told those who were still pure to move aggressively into the lives of those who had fallen, to snatch them from the fire and save them, all the while reacting with loathing to the very clothing they had worn while engaging in their immoral escapades.

Forever people—those of us who know that ultimately we are going to experience the eternal mercy of our heavenly Father—must be proactive and recognize our responsibility to live the way God wants us to live. Our behavior must have an aggressive, muscular quality as we do what must be done to remain in God's love. Yes, God loves us, but we too must do our part to remain in that love.

O God, as I wait to receive the fullness of your eternal mercy, help me to understand my responsibility to keep in your love. May I never forget what you have done and are doing for me. May I resist all temptation to dishonor you with my lifestyle. Hear me and help me for Jesus sake, Amen.

THIRTY-FIVE

Living in the Temple

*In [Christ Jesus] you too are being built together to
become a dwelling in which God lives by his Spirit.*
—Ephesians 2:22

In September of 1960, I began preaching a sermon on Ephesians 2:19-22 in the
Cottage Grove Christian Reformed Church of South Holland, Illinois. I completed the sermon thirty-eight years later in the same church. Obviously, I did a
lot of other things between the beginning and the end of that message.

I began preaching the sermon as a candidate for the ministry before a gathering
of preachers and elders who were responsible for judging whether I should be
ordained. The assembled brethren let me complete only about ten minutes of the
sermon before they signaled me to stop. That was, apparently, about all they could
take. In September 1998, thirty-eight years later, I preached the sermon in its
entirety when I assumed a position as a pastor of the very church in which I had
been examined earlier. Those who listened then were good enough to let me finish.

Over the years I have returned to this passage frequently because it describes the
nature of the church so brilliantly. We need its description of the church because
there are elements of ecclesiastical life that disenchant us. Sometimes necessary
denominational policies and structures get under our skin. Even more frequently,
our experience in the local church can be marred by sharp disagreements and inconsiderate behavior. Our country is full of men and women who ricochet from church
to church, remaining in each local body until something happens that troubles
them enough to send them off again in search of the ideal.

As a consequence, local churches that have been around for five years or so will
frequently be decimated by disagreements. Church members are often intense peo-

ple who do not have opinions about serious subjects, only convictions. As sometimes happens, their virtues become their vices. Their very commitment to the truth, which is exemplary, can make it impossible for them to appreciate another believer's variation on a theme. That is not exemplary.

In making these remarks, I point no finger; I am describing myself as a serious believer. Because we are the way we are, it is necessary to remind ourselves that the church is an object of our faith—as the Apostles' Creed puts it, "I believe in the holy catholic church." In spite of how we may feel about the local church of which we are members at the moment, we must teach ourselves always to look beyond the church in front of our nose to the church in front of our faith.

Ephesians 2 is talking about a church that goes far beyond our local church and denomination. This glorious church is the very bride of Christ. It is fundamentally a spiritual reality—the components of this building are divine revelation delivered through apostles and prophets, the exalted Lord Jesus Christ, who is the cornerstone—the person who defines the church through and through—and the Holy Spirit, who has made the church his dwelling place.

Not only is the church that is holy and catholic breathtakingly beautiful because the triune God is found within it, but also because its members are all of redeemed humanity. The church is the quantum leap from the Jewish nationalism of the Old Testament to the universal inclusiveness of people from every nation. The church is the fulfillment of all the promises to Abraham: all believers, regardless of race or nation, become sons of Abraham because of their faith.

The Father's feast table is now as big as everywhere, and those who earlier were aliens are not only citizens of the heavenly kingdom but actual children within God's household. There is nothing else like it in all creation. The church for which I waited thirty-eight years to complete my sermon is important because it is a local expression of this spiritual church. A local church is important only if it is an expression of the spiritual holy and catholic church. If a church becomes a club, if it abandons the holy and catholic faith, it is of no value whatsoever.

No one is ever going to find the perfect church in this world. It is folly to try to find a church that pleases us 100 percent. But when we join with a congregation that is part of the holy and catholic church, God requires us to be faithful members who use our gifts and talents to bring God glory where he has placed us.

Father, Son, and Holy Spirit, please enable us to see the glory of your church. And help us work hard within the church were we have been placed. May we exhibit the gifts of the Spirit as we live in this beautiful fellowship. In Christ's name, Amen.

THIRTY-SIX

Overcoming Our Brokenness

Make every effort to keep the unity of the Spirit through the bond of peace.
—Ephesians 4:3

For those who have read the Bible through more often than they can count, the biggest problem with Bible-reading is that they do not really see what's on the page. That is the reason so many Bible readers and believers have such unsatisfactory experiences within the church. If we would really read Ephesians 4:3—*really read it*—we believers would get along better than we do.

As it is, take any ten local churches and you might well discover that half of them are going through inner turmoil. Then take denominations that possibly honor the same confessional collection—there's a better than even chance that their snipers are taking aim not at their common enemy but at like-minded brothers and sisters on the other side of the creek.

Often there is enormous sadness among committed Christians because of divisions in the church. This is why Ephesians 4:3 is worthy of at least five minutes of our attention—it is not a sentence that should be read without reflection. The emphasis here is on the strenuous effort required if there is to be peace within the church. To be sure, the actual state of the church depends primarily on the work of God in the Spirit within the fellowship, but this word, inspired by the Spirit, is directed to members who need to realize that their efforts are part of the picture.

The verb that calls us to invest time and energy in the peace of the church, along with its cognates, is exceptionally muscular and strong. Membership in the church has nothing to do with hammocks; it has everything to do with athletics. And right here, we see why church fellowship often breaks down. Church members assume that it will come automatically—that they need do nothing more than lean back and enjoy it. This assumption comes from the underworld.

It is important to notice the bookends for the call to exert our energy and spare no effort in working for unity in the Spirit. The sentence preceding describes the personality traits that are the sine qua non of a good spirit within the church: "Be completely humble and gentle; be patient; bearing with one another in love." Humility, gentleness, patience, love—these are not traits we have by nature. Often believers assume that the cognitive elements of our lives are the most important. That's true—because it is essential that we know the truth. But one of the things we "know" when we become believers in Christ is that he wants us to be humble and gentle, which is pretty difficult to be.

Immediately after the call to give attention to the unity of the Spirit, there is a reminder of the attention that must be focused on the doctrinal side of Christianity: the one body, the one Spirit, the one faith, the one baptism, and the one God and Father of all. Each of these items demands that we make sure that the church is indeed built on the foundation of the apostles and prophets and is drawing its life from the Word of God, which reveals these to us.

Christians must be prepared to make every effort to insure that the message the church presents, the sacraments it administers, and the worship it brings to our one God is pure. There are bound to be differences in point of view regarding such matters, some of them amounting to a mere nuance, others potentially striking to the heart of biblical teaching, verging on heresy.

The call to make every effort to keep the unity of the Spirit requires at the very least that we be patient with each other with regard to our differences. Patience is a primary Christian virtue. Patience is required because working through matters of teaching can require lengthy time periods. The basic elements of Christian doctrine were defined precisely over centuries. When major questions arise, believers must be willing to work on them for many decades if necessary. Doing so is not a symptom of laziness but of our confidence that "we cannot do anything against the truth, but only for the truth" (2 Cor. 13:8). Ultimately the truth will prevail.

Ephesians 4:3 requires that every believer work hard at preserving the unity of the Spirit. This is a fundamental responsibility. The truth of God will be revealed and exalted among those who are gentle, humble, patient, and loving.

To you, O Glorious God, we come—there is no other God but you.
Make each of us more gentle, humble, patient and loving.
Forgive us for taking the unity of the church for granted. Help us
to be diligent and loving as we live among your people. In Christ, Amen.

THIRTY-SEVEN

The Church of the Firstborn

You have come . . . to the church of the firstborn, whose names are written in heaven.
—Hebrews 12:22-23

When I talked to Mark a couple of years ago about how maybe it would be a good idea if he would go to church, he respectfully told me that it was very difficult for him to get up on Sunday mornings, and, you know, in the afternoons the Bears play. He grinned because he realized that what he said didn't make a lot of sense. But then, my suggestion didn't make a lot of sense either. This spring, when we talked for the first time this year, he was grinning again. He told me about his newborn son. "And I'm going to church," he said. "Got to take my son to church, you know. And I found a preacher who keeps me awake; he's even kinda entertaining."

Firstborn sons will do that for dads. Our prayer circle is going to have to do some special praying for Mark: it would be great if he would begin to understand what he has gotten himself into. I hope his entertaining preacher is getting the message across about what the church actually is. Because the church has a lot to do with heaven.

This is why people who realize that they have an eternal destiny want to be a part of the church—it's a gymnasium where they can begin to practice for what they are going to do when life over there begins.

An exciting description of the church is found in Hebrews 12, where it is contrasted to the thunder, lightning, and smoke that terrified the people of Israel when they approached Mount Sinai, where they received the law of God. "You have not come to a mountain that can be touched and that is burning with fire. . . . But you have come to Mount Zion, to the heavenly Jerusalem, the city of the living God. You have come to thousands upon thousands of angels in joyful assembly, to the church of the firstborn, whose names are written in heaven" (vv. 18, 22-23).

This description of the church is enough to make your head spin. We see the church on earth as part of a heavenly reality—notice it is called "the heavenly Jerusalem." It is, as the apostle Paul declares in Galatians 4:26, "the Jerusalem that is above [that is] free."

And notice the angels in this description. If you want to be touched by an angel, go to a church that is true and living, one that is part of the great body of believers that stretches throughout the entire world and includes those who are already in heaven. Angels hover over this church and inhabit it.

Some organizations meet on Sunday and call themselves "church." But they are not really church. We have to watch out and make sure that we don't connect with such an organization. But churches where Christ is central and the Bible is preached faithfully, where songs are sent heavenward from faith-filled hearts, where the fellowship of love and caring is honest and strong—such a church is actually the earthly expression of a heavenly, eternal reality.

There is also something about the church that should appeal to all middle children. Notice that it is called "the church of the firstborn." Nowadays, there are books written about the impact our place in the family has on our personality. Middle children, for example, are supposed to be somewhat less aggressive than the eldest and a little less sure of their identity. Well, there will be no middle children in the heavenly church, the Jerusalem that is above.

In Bible times, family placement determined inheritance. If you were the firstborn son, you received an inheritance much, much greater than that of the second son and of any other son in the family. Jesus Christ is God's only Son, and everything that belongs to God belongs to him. Those who believe in Christ receive the same inheritance Christ receives. The church of the firstborn is the church in which every person has the rights of the firstborn son.

I wonder how long it will be before Mark begins to understand how glorious the church really is. He admitted to me that he doesn't make it every week, but his wife does—she makes sure his firstborn son gets there. My prayer is that Mark will learn to love Christ Jesus, God's firstborn son, so that he too will become a firstborn son of God whose name is written in heaven.

O Lord, there are so many people, good people, who really don't understand how important and glorious your church is. Be with Mark and many like him who are just finding out what it means to be part of the church. We are glad Mark's firstborn is bringing him to church. Now, please make Mark your firstborn. In your name, Amen.

THIRTY-EIGHT

The Un-cozy Church

*"Go and make disciples of all nations, baptizing them . . .
and teaching them to obey everything I have commanded you."*
—Matthew 28:19-20

A big word we often use when we talk about the church is *fellowship*. In a city full of lonely people, the church offers a place where we can find comfort and sympathy. Most of us want a church where we feel comfortable, where we can be comforted, and where we can occasionally comfort others.

It is true that the church is uniquely able to provide its members with a social experience that is heartwarming and profoundly encouraging. But when we think of the church the way Jesus thinks of it, we know there also has to be something about the church that keeps us off-balance, wondering what is going to happen next. After all, the church that now exists in time is going to exist forever and ever—and it has to act "eternal" even now.

What does that mean? It means that living churches should be un-cozy—that is, no church should ever develop a club-like atmosphere in which people who are very similar enjoy being together. It can easily happen that a church becomes very cozy for the people who attend it.

Most churches are dominated by a single social class and a single ethnic or racial group. And of course they always strive to have everyone agree on everything. Now, when you have one social class and one ethnic group, all agreeing not only on the great truths of Christianity but also on all the details of worship and spiritual life, everyone becomes very much at ease with everyone else. The trouble is that such churches are missing the excitement of a living church that is busy preparing its members for a fascinating eternity.

As we read the New Testament, we have to conclude that Jesus does not like cozy churches. Look at his last word to the church. Standing on the mountain of ascension, he told his church (represented by the disciples) that he wanted them to move out and disciple the nations of the world—not just an individual here and there, but actual nations. Boom! With this, Jesus threw a hand grenade into the center of the cozy church.

Nations, you understand, do not get along very well with each other. Read the bumper stickers. Some even declare the superiority of their kind of people over all others. Wars are usually fought between nations or tribes, between people who feel justified in killing other people because they are from another national group.

Churches tend to consist of people who are very similar to each other, and they tend to exclude those who are different from them. Why? There are lots of sociological reasons that explain it. But the main reason they become cozy groups is that they listen to Jesus' last word—the word he spoke before he ascended to heaven—only about once a year, usually when they have a special week set aside for missions.

The overpowering truth of the Bible is that Jesus Christ wants his bride—the church—to be made up of people from all the nations. Everything about his last word to his disciples underscores how important this is for him. It should be just as important for us today.

After Jesus takes us by the shoulders and turns us around so that we begin to look at the nations, the first thing he does is to tell us that all authority in heaven and on earth has been given to him. Then he says that he will accompany his church as they obey his commission. Just think of it: as we disciple the nations, Jesus will be right there with us!

Usually, when groups of believers consider Jesus' commission, they assume it means they should send missionaries overseas or at least to another community somewhere. Nonsense! That's part of it, of course, but the church's primary mission begins right at the edge of the local church. In fact, it is expressed right within it, within the worship service where the gospel is proclaimed.

Trouble is, as soon as a church becomes a mission church, it's not as cozy as we prefer. But stop and think about it. Remember that Christ has left his church behind to gather the nations into his eternal kingdom, and someday when we are all together enjoying the splendor of eternal life, we will discover a unity and love among the uncountable multitude that will make "cozy" seem like toothpaste in comparison.

Lord Jesus, please use us during our brief time in this world to make disciples of all nations. Do whatever you must with us and through us to accomplish your exalted goals. Give us grace to love all nations as you do. O Lord, thank you for promising to be right next to us as we carry out your mission. Amen.

THIRTY-NINE

Longing for Communion

"I have eagerly desired to eat this Passover with you before I suffer."
—Luke 22:15

Those who want a dispassionate God need not consider the Christian faith. The God of Christianity is a God of great emotion and feeling. The gospel record reports not only Jesus' actions but also his feelings. And Jesus of Nazareth is God incarnate.

Among the passages that report Jesus' emotions, his groanings and his tears, few describe their intensity more powerfully than Luke's recounting of Jesus' announcement to the apostles that he "eagerly desired" to eat the Passover with them. There is no precise English-language equivalent for the original here. Not only is the word for *desire* unusually strong, but the adverb that modifies it (which is a cognate of the verb) is unusually strong as well. Combine the two and you have Jesus expressing a depth of emotion we can scarcely imagine—"with deepest desire I have desired deeply" comes close.

What we have, then, is the Son of God describing his overpowering longing to eat the paschal meal with his disciples. What was it that made him feel as he did? Several considerations likely contributed to the intensity of his feeling. For one thing, he knew that this would be the final Passover, because he knew that within hours the need of animal sacrifice for human sin would be gone. His perfect blood would render obsolete all other blood for sin. His followers would never celebrate the Passover again.

Then too, he knew that at the end of the meal he would replace the Passover with another meal that would provide believers sacramental nourishment. Within moments after voicing his deep desire, he extended his hand to the apostle band with bread and wine between his fingers: "This is my body," he said, and "This is

84

my blood of the covenant." No more lambs, no more yearling goats, but a morsel of bread and a few sips of wine would create a mystical union between Christ Jesus and his people that would be as strong as eternal life.

And with this we know the vision of a heavenly reality danced in his mind—the marriage supper of the Lamb described in Revelation 19:9. As Jesus talked with his disciples, he envisioned the next time they would sit at table together, face to face. That eternal meal would be bathed in divine glory.

But whatever it was precisely that caused him to speak as intensely as he did, what should surprise us most is that Jesus wanted to eat the meal with his disciples, just a sentence before specifically called "apostles." As Jesus confides his deep emotion to his disciples, the emphasis falls on the fact that he deeply desired to eat with *them*. The use of the word *apostle* here tells us that Jesus viewed the men around him as the foundation of his church. Those who are living members of the church today must view Jesus' statement as an expression of longing to eat this meal with them.

What happened when the apostles sat with Jesus at the so-called "last supper" continues to happen when he meets with the church in the sacred meal he established in place of the Passover. That is the Lord's Supper, holy communion, the Eucharist. By whatever name, it remains after the Passover has been set aside; it is the blessed replacement, infinitely more effective and meaningful than the Passover, though admittedly not nearly so dramatic.

When we sit down at the holy board, we should tune our inner ears so that we can hear the Savior say, "With deepest desire, I have desired deeply to eat this with you." Such is our Savior. He is not one who accomplished what needed to be done to secure our salvation and then went his own heavenly way, with no further involvement in our insignificant lives. On the contrary, he accomplished our salvation so that he could continue to have fellowship with us. He longs to eat this meal with us.

If this is so, surely we should respond with similar strong emotion. Yet how many of us are able to say, "I long to commune with Christ at his sacramental table"? And how often do those who are more intensely spiritual cry out for the table of the Lord? We are so busy with other things. We are goal-oriented people for whom there will be time enough for spiritual realities in eternity.

There is something very wrong with us when we do not long to eat with the one who longs to eat with us . . . forever.

Christ Jesus, forgive our preoccupations, which we justify so easily but which keep us from longing to eat with you. Forgive us for being so unemotional about our faith. May we carve out time this day to meditate on your deep desire to be close to us so that we will long to be with you as well. In your name, Amen.

FORTY

Sustained by His Body

"This is my body."
—Matthew 26:26

O ur great joy as we journey toward our ultimate destiny is that we may already be united to Jesus Christ, who will be the center of our attention forever. He instituted a special meal that unites us to him—the sacrament of the Lord's Supper.

Just hours before he sacrificed his body on the cross Jesus said, "This is my body." He made a similar statement about the wine: "This is my blood of the covenant. . . . " What did he mean when he said these things? We must begin by believing that he meant what he said. "This is my body" is a simple sentence; each word is clear. He meant that the bread was his body and the wine was his blood.

But of course the bread has always remained bread, and the wine has always remained wine. Thankfully, that is true. So while these statements are straightforward enough, they were not, nor are they, literally true.

Not literally true. Nevertheless, they are true in a way that transcends literal meaning. Jesus is saying that when we partake of the elements of the supper, we are actually partaking of him, though we are doing so in a spiritual manner.

Earlier Jesus had talked about the necessity of eating his flesh and drinking his blood. Those teachings are recorded in John 6. This was uppermost in his mind; it was a major preoccupation as he approached the cross where his body would be mutilated and his blood poured out.

Over the years there have been a couple of ways believers have tried to explain what happens when they partake of the blessed supper. Some have said that even though the bread and the wine do not appear to change, they actually do change into the real body of Christ and his real blood. In this view, the morsels of bread, once they have been consecrated, become unusually precious and holy; no crumb may drop to the ground, nor may a drop of his blood be spilled.

Others have said that Jesus' body and blood surround the bread and the wine. His body, we are told, is everywhere; his glorified divinity is everywhere. Since the exalted Savior is once again the omnipresent God, his body is omnipresent too. Thus when we eat the bread and drink the wine in faith, we actually eat and drink the glorified, now omnipresent, body of Christ. His glorified body surrounds the elements.

Still others have rejected both of these explanations of Jesus' statement "This is my body." They have said that the Lord's Supper is a memorial; we eat the meal in remembrance of Christ. And surely this is an important part of the sacrament, for Jesus said, "This is my body, which is for you; do this in remembrance of me" (1 Cor. 11:24). But what we eat and drink is the body and blood of Christ—that is also what he said.

If we believe that the bread and wine are actually changed, we find ourselves working with a somewhat "magical" approach to the sacrament. If we believe that the physical body of Christ is present wherever Christ is present, we attribute to his physical body characteristics that are decidedly nonphysical.

Elsewhere I have referred to the Belgic Confession, Article 35, which emphasizes that when we partake of the sacrament by faith we are united to the glorified body of Christ, which is in heaven at the right hand of God the Father. The mystery then is not in the substance of the bread and wine, nor is it in the function of the bread and wine, which are alleged to carry Christ's body into our lives; the mystery is in the work of the Holy Spirit, who graciously unites us to the Lord when we partake in faith.

John Calvin's reaction to all this is extremely helpful: "It is a mystery of Christ's secret union with the devout, which is by nature incomprehensible. If anybody should ask me how this communion takes place, I am not ashamed to confess that that is a secret too lofty for either my mind to comprehend or my words to declare. And to speak more plainly, I rather experience than understand it."

The sacrament is a blessed means of grace that enhances our communion with Christ. As we journey to the place where we will be with him eternally, we are united to him already in this world. We are truly forever people, invulnerable to death itself because we are in the Living One and the Living One is in us.

Blessed Lord Jesus Christ, we thank you for the heavenly food and drink of life eternal, with which you graciously nourish us as we make our way toward glory. Help us to experience the wonder of this, though we can never understand your sacramental grace. Amen.

FORTY-ONE

Samuel's Grandson

Here are the men who served, together with their sons: . . .
Heman, the musician, the son of Joel. . . .
—1 Chronicles 6:33

I expect that after all Samuel's disappointment with Joel, Heman must have warmed his heart—that is, if Samuel ever got to hear him play his instruments and sing. Few people in Israel's history were more devoted to righteousness than Samuel the judge, but somehow Joel missed it: he took bribes and perverted justice. His son Heman got the family back on track. Heman was one of King David's great musicians; he had fourteen sons and three daughters who were part of the chorus that sang before the Lord after the Ark of the Covenant was returned to Jerusalem.

Those who take the time to read the two books of Chronicles will learn what was most important in Israel's life. In both books, there is a striking emphasis on musicians. In the sixth chapter of 1 Chronicles, the seemingly interminable genealogies slow down to a crawl and give us in-depth information about Israel's musicians—Heman; Asaph, his right-hand man; and the Merarites, who served on his left hand.

Throughout these books there are many special references to the singers and the players (see 1 Chron. 15, for example). We have reason to believe that they were men of spiritual depth who also provided the king with counsel. Clearly, the worship of God's ancient people featured music as a primary element.

Musicians were considered important enough to be singled out for special attention. When Heman appears, his disgraceful father is mentioned, and then his parentage is traced all the way back to Levi himself. The message is clear: Look at this man, this musician, and realize that he has been brought onto the scene and especially endowed with talents so that he can present the kind of music God wants in our worship.

Those who expect to spend eternity in heaven will want to be part of the church here on earth because it is a place where the people of God bring their music to the Lord. It happens in general worship when the people sing their praises together. It also happens when the gifted musicians of the church bring their tribute to God with voice and with their instruments.

So we see Heman, with that talented family of his, involved in the public praise of God. We see him with the other musicians who worked with him to make the place of worship a delightful place to be. But the delight that the music generates is not only enjoyed by the assembled worshipers. It is a delight that is wafted aloft into heaven's throne room.

When we think of musicians and choirs these days, we often think of the megachurches that assemble large choirs in their worship. "What is it that makes your church so popular?" I once asked a physician in Louisville, Kentucky. Without hesitation, he said, "Well, we have a glorious choir—three hundred voices." Great! But how many churches can have that kind of choir? Most of our churches are much, much smaller. Much.

Ah, yes, but even a smaller choir—say thirty members, maybe forty, maybe less—is just as important in a worship service. The books of Chronicles show us that the ministry of musicians is extremely significant. So the choir members come, perhaps an hour before the service, perhaps during the week, and they work hard to make their music excellent. Their ministry is worthy of all the effort they give it.

Some believers have been unusually gifted by the Lord with marvelous voices, or they are skilled instrumentalists. We need them all. We need to find a place for them. And as the assembled congregation listens to the music the musicians bring, they should think of it as a sacrifice brought to the Lord himself.

Now, a serious question. Heman was God's appointed musician, right? Do you think you would have appreciated his music? Likely, it was very different from ours today. The truth is that different cultures have different music—there's no getting around that. As the church becomes more and more diverse, believers have to learn to appreciate one another's music.

Praise the Lord . . . with the trumpet, harp, lyre, tambourine, and dancing, with the strings and the flute, the clash of cymbals. "Let everything that has breath praise the Lord" (Ps. 150:6).

Heman, please lead the way for us.

O Lord, you have made this world delightful and your church especially so. Thank you for creating music and for giving special talents to your children. Make us people who sing and play our best when we praise you now and forever. In Christ, Amen.

FORTY-TWO

Jumpin' Jehoshaphat!

Instantly, the man's feet and ankles became strong.
He jumped to his feet and began to walk.
—Acts 3:7-8

an believers still expect miracles? Sure they can. But they should not expect miracles like those reported in the New Testament when Jesus and his apostles were around. Not like what happened when Jehoshaphat jumped to his feet.

In earlier times people used the expression "Jumpin' Jehoshaphat!" to express surprise. Seems like an expression you might find in Mark Twain, like the "Celebrated Jumping Frog of Calaveras County." Jehoshaphat could have been the name of the man Peter and John healed—he could have been named after the celebrated king of Judah. Let's give him that name as we think about him.

Miracles are always astounding, but when Jehoshaphat jumped to his feet, even the men who sent Jesus to the cross had to sit up and take notice. They had to admit it: "Everybody living in Jerusalem knows [Jesus' followers] have done an outstanding miracle, and we cannot deny it" (Acts 4:16). Even today, as we look back along the centuries at the report of what happened to this man, we cannot keep from shaking our heads in amazement. No, we don't have miracles like this anymore.

Jehoshaphat was more than forty years old when the energy shot like an electric shock into his legs, which he had never used his entire life. Think of how this man must have looked. Likely the upper part of his body had developed; his arms and chest might have been strong because of the way he had to move himself around with them—like a wheelchair "runner" in the Chicago Marathon. But the muscles of his legs were not all that much different from what they were when the midwife cleaned him up and gave him to his mother. He had never walked!

Acts 3 and 4 emphasize that his healing was instantaneous. One minute he was sitting there, as he had for most of his forty years, waiting for a few coins to live on; the next minute he was on his feet. Peter's assistance was virtually unnecessary. As Peter and John entered the temple courts, Jehoshaphat walked and jumped beside them. Everybody knew this man, and everybody could see that God was at work.

Oh, it was God all right. And let us be specific about this, said Peter. It is Jesus' name and the faith that comes through him that have given complete healing to this man. *Complete* healing—that's what makes this miracle unique.

Up until this day, all his life Jehoshaphat had been a spectacle of powerless infirmity, reminding everyone who came to the temple that there was something dreadfully wrong with God's creation. He had learned to bear his misery, and the people had become accustomed to seeing him sit there. Often they would look right through him or past him. He knew their glances. Then, in a heartbeat, he was transformed totally. He stood up, he jumped, he praised God. The people gazed at Jehoshaphat open-mouthed and uncomprehending.

Miracles nowadays are different. Usually they occur in the context of some form of healing, medicine or alternative medicine of some sort. People resort to medical treatments and pray fervently that God will use it, and God does use it. Praise God for his grace! In some cases, reports of a miraculous healing are surrounded by events that make us doubt somewhat; we can never be sure. This doesn't mean that they do not still happen, but we can never be sure. God cares for us and heals some of us beyond our wildest dreams, and we do thank him for these signs of grace. But they are different from what happened to Jehoshaphat.

What happened to him was complete; it was instantaneous. And (this is the good part) it is unquestionably reliable—we read it in the Bible. This event actually happened, no question about it. There is no hysteria here. The report is accurate and precise. Let none of our current miraculous events ever be compared with this one.

As we see Jehoshaphat jumping beside the apostle, we realize that this Jesus we believe in is indescribably powerful. He is alive, and the day will come when all who trust in Jesus will be healed. "Then will the eyes of the blind be opened and the ears of the deaf unstopped. Then will the lame leap like a deer, and the mute tongue shout for joy" (Isa. 35:5-6).

JUMPIN' JEHOSHAPHAT!

Risen, ascended Lord Jesus Christ, Savior with the powerful name, we praise you for your healing power. We long for the day when a great miracle like this will happen in our lives—when our death-trapped bodies will be perfect like yours. May it happen soon, O Jesus! Amen.

FORTY-THREE

When Forever Began

In the beginning God created the heavens and the earth.
—Genesis 1:1

The Bible summons us to look ahead, way ahead, into our forever and God's forever. But as we do that, questions arise about when forever began. Nowadays scientists have initiated projects—including space probes and a new mapping of the universe—in an attempt to discover information about the beginning of everything.

The forever the Bible describes, an eternity in the presence of God in joyful service of the Lamb of God, Christ Jesus, had a beginning. For those who believe the Bible's record, the beginning is very different from physicist Steven Weinberg's description of the universe a fraction of a second before the "big bang." In *The First Three Minutes* Weinberg writes:

> At very early times the universe could be considered to consist of photons, leptons, antileptons, quarks and antiquarks, all moving essentially as free particles, and each particle species therefore in effect furnishing just one more kind of black-body radiation. It is easy then to calculate that there must have been a beginning, a state of infinite density *and* infinite temperature, about one-hundredth of a second before the first frame.

Such language has its own fascination, but for those who believe the Scriptures, it represents yet another attempt to avoid what Weinberg calls the "problem of Genesis." Those whose hope for an eternal existence of heightened joy and achievement rests upon data found in the Scriptures must find the answers to our questions about the origin of both the universe and of humanity in Genesis—the place the Bible begins.

"In the beginning God created the heavens and the earth"—that the Bible begins with this statement seems entirely natural and fully appropriate for those who have long known this book. But religious books often begin differently; and the Bible could have begun very differently. That it begins with a statement about origins is a powerful declaration that whatever we believe about our future must be based entirely on what we know about the beginnings of the universe, of this planet, and of our race.

It is folly to try to understand who we are and where we are going without believing the first verses of the Bible. It is folly to relegate this material to mythology similar to the Norse view of the way the world began. In the opening pages of the Bible, we find what we need to know about the beginning of forever.

For God, of course, forever has no beginning because God is the only eternal reality. When we attempt to think of God, we almost immediately run out of words and concepts that might enable us to understand what it would mean for a personal being to have no beginning and no ending. But we do know this: God created us in his image, which means that we will exist forever as God does, though our forever began with time and God's did not.

So when did forever begin for us? It began in the beginning. And the Bible, which speaks of that distant moment, does not then drop the subject; it goes on to give us information about the way the eternal God gave the formless universe a structure that continues to endure. Interestingly, Steven Weinberg, in spite of his fear of the book of Genesis, nonetheless asserts that at the very beginning there was only radiation, or to put it differently, there was only light. So too the Bible describes the first day—there was only light.

And so the days move forward. Were they twenty-four hour days? As far as we are concerned, they were, for God's moral law is built on the rhythm of six days of labor and one of rest. We must not forget, however, that the creation account reports the work of the eternal God who, needless to say, does not wear a Rolex. God is eternal and sovereign—God does as he pleases, when he pleases. And in the days of creation Genesis describes, we see the progression God wants us to remember.

Eternal people must always begin to understand themselves by beginning at the beginning described in first three chapters of the book of Genesis. God's revelation is all we need, and it begins at our beginning.

O Sovereign Creator God, from whom all things have come, we bow in meek humility as part of your majestic creation. Your creation is as incomprehensible as your own being. Receive our praise and forgive us too, in Jesus' name. Amen.

FORTY-FOUR

See the Rainbow

"I have set my rainbow in the clouds, and it will be the sign of the covenant between me and the earth."
—Genesis 9:13

I had never before seen my scientist friend so excited. He was telling me about what he'd seen in Hawaii—a rainbow caused not by the sun but by the moon. This rainbow was created by the brilliant rays of the full moon shining on the mist left behind by an evening storm. Apparently this happens very, very seldom, and he was ecstatic to have seen it.

Although most of us will never see a rainbow like the one my friend saw, we do see a rainbow from time to time. I saw one early in the morning a couple of days before I wrote this. It was barely light, and it hadn't even rained. There were dark clouds in the west, and the light of the rising sun put a brilliant crescent of color over my head. I must confess that although I enjoyed the color, it didn't move me all that much. I didn't even mention it to anyone.

If we would live more fully by the Bible, we would be more moved by rainbows than we are. Seeing a rainbow would be enough to make us catch our breath and think, "There is the glorious finger of God telling of his mercy."

In Genesis 9 we learn that God put the rainbow in the heavens as a covenant sign. This chapter gives the impression that there had never been rainbows before. The biblical record allows for this idea. In fact, when we read about the universal flood that destroyed every creature that breathes, with the exception of those who were with Noah in the ark, we might also conclude that there had been no rain before the flood judgment.

Those who have a uniformitarian view of history would reject the idea that the earth was different before the flood from what it was afterward. Genesis 2:6 gives

94

the impression that before the flood the earth was watered by water that came from within the earth, not by water that fell from the sky. The King James Version translates the verse by saying that the earth was watered by a mist that came from within it. And the Bible says explicitly that after the flood, God set a rainbow in the clouds for a specific purpose. It would forever after serve as a sign of God's grace.

A rainbow is impressive because it is as much a sign for God as it is for us. God told Noah that he would set the rainbow in the clouds so that whenever he saw it, he would remember his covenant with Noah. A covenant is a promise. God promised never again to destroy the world with a flood. The rainbow is the string on God's finger that always reminds him of this promise.

Likely Noah and his little company were the first to see a rainbow, and ever after, when he saw it, he remembered that God was looking at it too. The brilliant sign stretched across the sky is by no means merely nature's commonplace.

Within the church, there has always been discussion about the frequency of the sacraments—like the rainbow, reminders of God's grace. Just as the sacraments are covenantal signs and seals of God's covenant of grace, the rainbow is the sign of God's covenant with all living things. And what of the frequency of this covenant sign? It is as frequent as sunshine follows rain. God's people look up and see the rainbow's gorgeous colors and remember that all the forces of nature are under divine control. We journey into forever in a world that is carefully controlled by our Sovereign and merciful God. God's wrath is enormous and, when unleashed, wreaks havoc everywhere. But each time we observe this marvelous sign, we are assured that we are living in a day of grace. God has arranged for nature itself to cooperate with his gracious intent.

Like the wren that chirps while building her springtime nest in our birdhouse, all of us puny creatures are living in a time in which God controls the fall of every leaf and the energy of the wildest tornado, making sure that seedtime and harvest will surely continue until the Savior comes. In this place, safe from worldwide desolation, followers of the coming Christ may prepare for the judgment of fire that will finally come by telling the message of salvation through the cross of Calvary.

Our rainbows spur us on . . . while there's still time.

O God of judgment, make our faith so sensitive that we will always look at the rainbow's announcement of your control of all creation. Please continue to withhold your judgment so that more people may flee to your mercy. Amen.

FORTY-FIVE

The James Factor

[Herod] had James, the brother of John, put to death with the sword.
—Acts 12:2

Most of us have a calculator in our minds to establish the appropriate timetable for our lives. We expect that most people will live long enough to make their lives worthwhile. When Wayne, one of my classmates in seminary, died about the same time the rest of us graduated, it seemed a waste that he had prepared for the ministry but never had a chance to serve.

Same goes for James. It has always puzzled me that he died so soon—he was the first of Jesus' disciples to be martyred. If it had been Andrew I could understand, because Andrew was a very ordinary disciple. But James was especially prepared for a very productive apostleship. He was one of only two other disciples who were exceptionally close to Jesus.

In fact, James and his brother John were likely Jesus' cousins. John 19:25 and Matthew 27:53 indicate that James's mother, Salome, the wife of Zebedee, was Jesus' mother's sister. Often when Jesus and his disciples were on the road together, James's mother was with them. She probably took care of her boys' laundry. Jesus went out of his way to take James and John, along with Peter, with him at the high points of his ministry. These three were with Jesus when he raised Jairus's daughter from the dead and when he was transfigured on the mountain. James was close to Jesus in the Garden of Gethsemane. While most of the disciples remained at the garden entrance, James, John, and Peter accompanied Jesus deep among the olive trees. Likely, James heard Jesus cry out in agony as he saw the full horror of the wrath-filled cup.

After all this, James was the first to go to heaven, probably about ten years after Jesus' ascension, maybe eleven. When he did, he found out how preposterous his request to sit next to Jesus in glory had been. It had happened as Jesus was headed to Jerusalem to be crucified. Although James's mother made the request, James and his brother were in on it from the start. "Grant that one of these two sons of mine may sit at your right and the other at your left in your kingdom," she said to Jesus (Matt. 20:21).

James was a courageous fighter, actually. He and his brother were not called "Sons of Thunder" for nothing. James was quick to identify Jesus' enemies and quick to strike out at them. He and John once suggested that a Samaritan village that did not want Jesus to pass through be set afire (Luke 9:54). After Jesus' ascension James became well-known as a partisan of the Savior, so when Herod killed him with a sword, possibly publicly, the Jewish establishment applauded.

James did not serve long, but he served well. Thinking about him gives us perspective on our own lives and the lives of others. We may be sure that when Herod's executioner dispatched James, his Savior was not surprised. In fact, on the very day James longed to forget—the day he and John had made their move toward a throne—Jesus acknowledged that they would be baptized with a baptism similar to his own. Jesus knew that James would die a violent death, and he knew when it would occur. Obviously, there is no guarantee that those who prepare themselves for special service in the God's kingdom will serve for a normal life span. There is no guarantee that especially gifted children will live long enough to use their talents. There is no human equation that yields information about the length of our days and of our service.

It's all up to Jesus. He said as much the day he talked with Peter about Peter's death, and Peter looked over at James's brother John and said, "What about him?" Jesus replied: "If I want him to remain alive until I return, what is that to you? You must follow me" (John 21:22).

And that's the way it is with each of our lives. We must just follow Jesus. We must do what God wants us to do today—what *God* wants us to do. We serve at his pleasure. That's what James did. Maybe he thought Herod would never touch him because Jesus had trained him so well. Possibly he was so brave because he thought God would give him special protection. He found out otherwise. And we may be sure it all makes sense to him now as he serves Christ in glory.

Lord Jesus, what a privilege you give us as you call us to serve you in various ways. You train us all differently and equip us all differently. May we use the gifts you've given in your service in this day, confident that you will let us serve you here as long as you determine. We trust you. Amen.

FORTY-SIX

Recognizing Jesus

Thinking he was the gardener, she said,
"Sir, if you have carried him away, tell me. . . . "
—John 20:15

O ne of the mysteries that surrounds the resurrected Lord Jesus Christ is this: apparently, when he rose from the dead, his appearance was somewhat different from what his followers remembered. Mary's failure to recognize him at once is an especially touching illustration of mistaken identity. The gardener? She thought he must be the gardener!

The case of two of Jesus' followers, whom he accompanied as they walked to Emmaus together, recorded in Luke 24, is also puzzling. It is especially problematic because of the extended time they spent with one another. Their discussion was not only lengthy but fairly complicated. "Beginning with Moses and all the Prophets, he explained to them what was said in all the Scriptures concerning himself" (v. 27). Not until later, however, when Jesus duplicated the same words and motions he had used frequently among them—when he took bread, gave thanks, and gave it to them—did they recognize him.

As we consider this information, we should set our puzzlement aside. Of course they didn't recognize Jesus immediately! How could they? Think of it this way. All of those who failed to identify Jesus had been very close to him; most, if not all of them, had witnessed his crucifixion. When his body was prepared for burial, "all those who knew him, including the women who had followed him from Galilee, stood at a distance, watching these things" (Luke 23:49). This means that strong visual images of the crucifixion of Christ had been burned into their minds.

When people die, they are transformed. Those who observe a loved one dying over a period of several weeks will notice that the cheeks become hollow; a few days before death, the eyes begin to sink into the skull. With Jesus the dying process was hastened by the trauma of the crucifixion. Think how horrible that was. Whereas the final care of the dying seeks to protect the body of the dying person as much as possible, crucifixion is the very opposite. It is literally an excruciating death; Jesus' body was pierced and mutilated; a crown of thorns laid streaks of clotted blood across his forehead and cheeks. When Joseph of Arimathea and Nicodemus removed Jesus' lifeless body from the cross, the corpse was a physical catastrophe.

And remember what they did to him then. Once he breathed his last, his followers seemed to think of one thing: spices. Nicodemus, dear man, came to the crucifixion site with a seventy-five-pound bag of spices. The women went home and prepared the spices and perfumes they took to the tomb on the day of resurrection. At the crucifixion site, Nicodemus and Joseph wrapped Jesus' body. If they used all seventy-five pounds of spices, what they eventually laid into the tomb must have resembled a cocoon more than a human form. It must have been a very heavy load to lift; if Jesus weighed 150 pounds, once they were finished, the body they laid in the tomb weighed about 225 pounds.

All of this contributed to visual images that remained fixed in Jesus' followers' minds. They couldn't erase the crucifixion scene from their minds; nor could they shake the picture of those who worked over his body, wrapping it in seemingly endless strips of linen, laying spices between the folds. Only his head emerged from all this cloth and spice, wrapped in a solitary head covering. So there was little connection between the glorified Christ who appeared to them on resurrection day and the corpse they had put into the tomb. Besides, Jesus wore clothing that had come from God. He was placed into the tomb virtually naked, his clothing having been casinoed away by legionnaires. Where did he get his robe? It could only have come from the same place that the first clothing of our first parents came from: God must have made it for him. Likely it was different from what he had worn earlier.

Jesus may even have walked with a different gait; after all, he did not really have to walk at all with that glorified body of his that could suddenly appear among his disciples, and as quickly disappear.

As we read the gospels, we learn that it was ultimately Jesus' wounds that identified him. His wounds. From then on he would be known as the Lamb of God. When he shows us his wounds we know him, not before. Then we are sure that he is alive. Then we are sure that we, along with him, will be alive forevermore.

O Lamb of God, who takes away the sin of the world, remove from
our feeble minds any representation of your glorified body.
May we simply remember that in your glory, we are assured
that someday we too will be glorified beyond imagining. Amen.

FORTY-SEVEN

How Many Angels?

As [Mary] wept, she bent over to look into
the tomb and saw two angels in white. . . .
—John 20:12

When we read the reports of Jesus' resurrection, we discover several angels. Matthew speaks of one angel who rolled back the tombstone and sat on it, scaring the guards to death. Mark tells us that the women found a "young man dressed in a white robe sitting on the right side" when they looked in the tomb. Luke tells of two angels who talked to the women as they came to the tomb, and John describes two angels in white sitting where the body of Jesus had been, one at the head and one at the foot.

Just how many angels were there? Were there just two: the one who rolled the stone away and a companion? Or were there more: the one who sat on the stone, the two who talked to the women, the one who talked to the women, and the two who sat at the foot and head of the place where Jesus' body had been placed? That would be six.

However many there were, it's fascinating that they conversed with the women who came to the tomb. Biblical religion is supernatural religion; heaven keeps touching earth. If a person doesn't believe that the realm of heaven touches the realm in which we live, that person can't really be a Christian.

But let's get back to our question: How many angels were there? It's possible to look at them and try to enumerate them, as I did earlier. But when we look at the total biblical revelation regarding angels, it is more than likely that there were angels all over the place when the women came to the tomb.

Angels, after all, are not "there" only when we see them. We see them when they are revealed to us. They are ministering spirits whom God sends out to accomplish his mission. And angels were very close to Christ throughout his earthly ministry.

When Jesus was born, angels filled the sky with heaven's glory. When the devil left him after tempting him, angels came and ministered to him; we get the impression that there were several of them. And an angel came and strengthened him when he was in the Garden of Gethsemane.

According to the biblical data, angels had a deep interest in what Christ was doing, every step of his earthly journey. There is every reason to think that the angels who are identified in the accounts of Jesus' resurrection—the one on the tombstone and the two who talked to the women in the tomb, for example—were just a few of a host of angels on the scene at the time.

In fact, when we think about the profound significance of Jesus' suffering and death and resurrection, it is more than likely that there were many angels nearby as the women approached the tomb. Angels were likely present at all of the great resurrection events described in the gospels. They attended to many of the details.

Admittedly this is speculation, but it is speculation supported by the thrust of the Scriptures. One thing is sure: Angels are real and they are involved whenever anything truly important occurs in God's great salvation plan. We can be sure that when the trumpet sounds and Christ returns, there will be angels galore.

In any case, when Christ arose from the dead, it's very possible that there were many angels on the scene, praising God for his great work of salvation, but only a few of them were revealed to the women and talked with them.

But for us it's even more important to think about the angels that are here.

The spiritual realm is real, and it is not out beyond Mars somewhere. It's very close. There are fallen angels, and there is evidence that they are very active. And there are holy angels. They are very interested in us, and they are especially interested in our faith. How and why and when God uses them in our lives, we can never say for sure. But we may be sure that they exist, and in special times of danger they often intervene so that our lives are spared.

Resurrection Day was a good day for angels. We, who live in the power of the resurrection, should believe that if ever a time comes when we need angel care, God will send us one . . . or two . . . or twenty . . . or two hundred . . . thousand!

Risen Lord, we are encouraged by the way your angels talked to the women at the tomb. There is so much about angels we do not know, but help us think about them more, and help us trust you to send angels to help us whenever it's necessary. Amen.

FORTY-EIGHT

Living by Faith

"The righteous will live by faith."
—Romans 1:17

T he biblical statement that the righteous will live by faith has caused cataclysmic change. Probably the greatest event it caused was the Protestant Reformation, which changed the world. It happened when Martin Luther suddenly understood that the righteous will live by faith.

For him that meant that the righteous would be delivered from hell through faith in the finished work of Jesus Christ. As Abraham believed God, and it was reckoned to him for righteousness, so believers today believe that what God has promised us in Jesus Christ is surely true, and we receive eternal life.

We must take the verb *live* in the sentence *The righteous will live by faith* very seriously. It does not mean only that those who believe in the Lord Jesus Christ will be delivered from damnation and will live eternally; it also means that during their days on earth, they will live each day by faith.

The apostle Paul writes about this in 2 Corinthians 5:7: "We live by faith, not by sight." Once we believe in the Lord Jesus Christ, and once the Bible, which reveals Jesus, becomes the authority in our life, everything in our life must be under the control of Christ and his Word.

This is what it means to be "forever" people. Forever people do not think of themselves as temporary beings who have just so many days to live, so we had better make the most of them. Some people try to get around such a bleak view of themselves by believing in reincarnation. Good try—but it happens to be false. Even Christian believers sometimes view their lives in this world as being disconnected from whatever future the Bible talks about.

Sadly, some believers fall into the trap of thinking that they can engage in a certain amount of sin that they happen to enjoy. God will forgive them, they think, and eternity is plenty long enough time to be perfect. They do not see a direct connection between eternal life and their temporal lives. They fail to understand that if they are believers, they are already living their eternal life. They have faith, but they don't live by it. This is high tragedy.

Sometimes people wonder if they have true, saving faith. The best way to tell if they have it is to ask themselves whether or not they are living by faith now . . . right now. To be honest, none of us live by faith to the degree that we should. But to be a believer is to work at growing in grace and learning to live this way. In this life, we can make a beginning at living by faith, not by sight. "The righteous will live by faith."

Being a forever person who lives each day by faith, not by sight, is a very satisfying experience. It is a way of life that is sustained by the presence of Christ and the power of his Holy Spirit. It is the life of prayer and of regular communion with God through the reading and study of the Bible. It is a life of fellowship with other Christians who are also seeking to live by faith. It is a truly beautiful and wholesome life.

These days, it's easy to get the idea that we are Christians if we conform to a certain lifestyle. Each church and each church community has its characteristic lifestyle—this is inevitable. Sometimes we give one another the impression that we are truly Christian people if we act like others in our church. As a result, many people never discover what it means to live each day in the light of Christ and of eternity.

"The just shall live by faith." When speaking of this text, Martin Luther would always add the word *alone:* "The just shall live by faith *alone.*" Forever people say it this way: "The righteous will live every moment of every day by faith."

Living by faith every moment of every day enables us to live in the light of eternity. Living this way is really living. It is living a life that will never end. Although our lives will be different when we get to glory, already now we can live for our Savior, who once told us that if we believe in him, we will never die.

Living Lord Jesus Christ, help us to live this day, every moment, by faith, not by sight. May we always remember that we are eternal people. May we be kind to others, diligent in our duty, and always aware of your merciful presence. We pray in your name, Amen.

FORTY-NINE

Craps

*You made him a little lower than the heavenly beings
and crowned him with glory and honor.*
—Psalm 8:5

The other day I discovered why gambling has swept this country like wildfire in New Mexico. I found the clue in the report of a high-level scientific conference dealing with human consciousness. David Chalmers upset everyone when he declared that it is impossible to explain human consciousness in terms of the mechanics of the brain. What got everyone so angry was that, if he is right, then there must be something like a soul—a "nonmaterial human essence." Come now, let's get serious.

Serious those scientists most certainly were. And they had to admit that they had more questions than answers. In fact, one of the participants, Colin McGinn, who wrote a book called *The Mysterious Flame,* said that he feels that evolution has designed our minds so that we cannot explain intelligence.

When I read that in *U.S. News and World Report,* I nearly fell out of my chair. Fortunately, it was an easy chair with strong arms to keep me in place. But McGinn was saying that evolution has "designed" us and our consciousness. Get that? *Designed.* Now, evolution cannot design anything. Evolution is strictly chance. That is all. So McGinn is saying that you and I are the product of a cosmic craps game.

Why is gambling so popular? Because somewhere along the line, a majority has concluded that everything we see around us is the result of a craps game. Craps is ultimate reality. Our ability to think has been "designed" by evolution, and anything that is so designed has to be a product of chance, nothing else.

I can well remember the craps games in the barracks. I can still see the guys playing. I remember the sharp expulsion of air from their mouths when the dice fell on

104

seven and eleven. Everyone would shout. There was great tension, especially on payday when the GIs thought they might make a few more bucks. As I listened to the excitement and occasionally wandered over and watched, I never thought I'd live to see the day when humankind would conclude that we have been designed by evolution—that the fall of cosmic dice determined what we are.

With the growing popularity of gambling and the idea of natural evolution as the ultimate explanation for all reality, including human consciousness, believers must realize that their position is generally viewed as nonsense. Our faith knowledge tells us that it is most certainly true that we cannot explain human consciousness in terms of the mechanics of the brain alone. We do have a soul; the Bible makes this very clear. The soul—often called the *heart* in the Bible—is the nonmaterial essential part of every human being. This soul has been created by the God who is an immaterial being. God is a spiritual being, and God has made us in his image. We are essentially spiritual beings too, not physical beings, because we are reflections of the being of God.

Believers who live in terms of eternity are a strange and peculiar community in the eyes of the majority, not just because of lifestyle, but because they experience life and all of reality differently from the way those who believe in the cosmic craps game experience it. For us, every moment is wonderful with importance, and every action occurs because of God's good and perfect guidance. Every action contributes to a glorious and marvelous future.

So the learned men and women gather. They deliver papers and make statements, they scratch their heads and become upset with one another as they seek to unravel the mystery of what they call human consciousness. They are confronted at every turn by data that indicates that human beings have souls, but they cannot accept *that;* they can accept anything but that. And so they conclude that all reality is an enormous craps game—the dice were thrown over and over again and the physical universe became what it is; thrown some more and my amaryllis was designed, and the finch that darts across the yard; thrown some more and human beings came into existence—creatures who love and care for one another and who worship—yes, they even worship, poor things.

God has made us a little lower than the angels. If only they would open God's book and read what's there. Then they would know. Then they would worship with us.

Creator God, eternal Mind and consciousness, we stand in awe as we
observe all that you have made. Humble us and our children,
and use us to bring your truth into this shamefully confused world
so that we may know our origin and destiny. In Christ, Amen.

FIFTY

Meaningful Meaningless Lives

"Utterly meaningless! Everything is meaningless."
—Ecclesiastes 1:2

It was supposed to hit sixty-six degrees by noon. I was encouraged as I drove to the Bible study and prayer group scheduled to start at 6:30 that morning; it sure hadn't been sixty-six as I shivered while putting gas in the car. I wondered who would lead and what Bible passage we would study. When I found out, it looked as if I could forget the day's promise.

"Meaningless! Meaningless!" says the Teacher. "Utterly meaningless! Everything is meaningless." The book of Ecclesiastes—what a way to begin the day! Kent, who was leading, forced us to read the first three chapters aloud, and then we talked about them.

Ecclesiastes describes the lifestyle of King Solomon, the king of Judah and Israel who started out great, but whose life flamed out after several years. He was the wisest man in the world; he built great palaces and the magnificent temple for Jehovah in Jerusalem; but he was also extremely self-indulgent, leading a sensuous lifestyle that included a harem (2:8). "I denied myself nothing my eyes desired; I refused my heart no pleasure" (2:10). The Teacher (the speaker in Ecclesiastes) says that he took great delight in his work, yet "When I surveyed all that my hands had done and what I had toiled to achieve, everything was meaningless, a chasing after the wind; nothing was gained under the sun" (2:11).

Thankfully, as we worked through those first three chapters that morning, we found nuggets of meaning—little phrases that indicated that it wasn't all ashes for the Teacher. We were finally rescued from total depression by a principle of Bible study that everyone who picks up the Bible ought to know about. It's called *progressive revelation.*

As we read the Bible and let it form our lives while we are moving toward the full experience of eternal life, this principle must always guide our understanding. If we didn't use it, the truth of the book of Ecclesiastes could drive us to despair: its description of the futility of life is right on target. For example, it talks frequently about the way people work their tails off to get ahead and end up having to leave everything behind. "I must leave [all the things I toiled for] to the one who comes after me. And who knows whether he will be a wise man or a fool?" (2:18-19). Ecclesiastes also describes the flip side of wisdom and knowledge: "With much wisdom comes much sorrow; the more knowledge, the more grief" (1:18).

After reading material like that for fifteen minutes or so, starting at 6:30 in the morning, we felt like climbing back into bed and starting over. But progressive revelation revived us. We reminded one another that Ecclesiastes is only part of the story. The Bible does not fudge on how dismal and grim life is without Jesus Christ. The Teacher knew about God, but he didn't know about Christ. When Christ came, he brought a salvation that not only turns people aside from the path to hell but also fills their ordinary days with meaning.

Exhibit number one is the apostle Paul's encouraging message to slaves: "Slaves, obey your earthly masters in everything; and do it, not only when their eyes are on you and to win their favor, but with sincerity of heart and reverence for the Lord. Whatever you do, work at it with all your heart, as working for the Lord, not for men, since you know that you will receive an inheritance from the Lord as a reward. It is the Lord Christ you are serving. Anyone who does wrong will be repaid for his wrong, and there is no favoritism" (Col. 3:22-25).

Progressive revelation—there is a progressive splendor in the Bible's message, a progressive clarity as we observe the grim ugliness of certain parts of the Old Testament falling away to be replaced by the call to give our entire lives as living sacrifices to God. Those who believe in Christ and who have Christ's Spirit in their heart do not live meaningless lives. Every element of their lives is infused with eternal significance.

As we finished our study, Kent reminded us of 1 Timothy 6:6: "Godliness with contentment is great gain." So it is. There is no need for us to be cynical about our humble lives. As we filed from the restaurant that morning, the day seemed filled with promise once again. Maybe it would actually hit sixty-six by noon.

O God, how empty and futile our lives are without you! Thank you for sending the Spirit of the living Christ into our hearts and making our lives worthwhile. Help us to see all we do today in the light of eternity. Make our day joyful and holy. In Christ, Amen.

FIFTY ONE

T4G = T4H

Train yourself to be godly.
—1 Timothy 4:7

As spiritual as it is, the New Testament contains a surprising number of references to athletic events. The apostle Paul was especially impressed by athletic
games. Possibly he would have subscribed to *Runner's World* if it had been
around.

Then again, he might not have. Likely he got plenty of exercise. He was a world
traveler—sometimes he used a ship and sometimes a horse or donkey, but he also
must have done a lot of walking. If anyone had shown him a stair stepper, he probably would have laughed.

Even so, he and his contemporaries were well aware of the rigorous training of ath-
letes. In writing to Timothy, Paul makes a striking comparison between athletic training and training for godliness. With all the emphasis on exercise nowadays, few would
suggest parallels between physical fitness and spiritual fitness, physical training and
spiritual training. These seem to be poles apart. But actually, they are very similar.

Readers of *Runner's World* know it's about how runners should live in order to
run well. It's about nutrition and diet supplements. It's about posture while running. It's about a weekly schedule, setting a mileage goal, and carving out blocks of
time to achieve that goal. It's about injuries—how to avoid them and what to do
when you get them. Those who are serious about their physical fitness take on a
way of life that reflects their interest twenty-four hours a day.

In his letter to his friend Timothy, the apostle makes a very simple point: physical training is okay, but godliness training is better. Physical training we can understand, but godliness training—what is that?

Godliness comes up fairly frequently in the Bible. In 1 Timothy it comes up again in the sixth chapter—"godliness with contentment is great gain." Since the apostle makes godliness a spiritual reality that is parallel to what happens when an athlete is in training, we should think of it as something that can be developed over time.

It follows from this that believers who are not in training will have less godliness than those who are. Possibly this is the reason for the great variation among believers in terms of the way they express their faith in daily life. Some believers are lethargic and lazy when it comes to developing godliness. They don't get much out of public worship and attend infrequently. They pray only when they have a personal crisis; they are very self-centered and they do a lot of thinking about material things. All of us have to admit that there is a streak of this lethargy in us. Just as it takes a special act of the will to follow a physical training regimen (actually hundreds of acts of will), it takes the same acts of will for training in godliness.

Godliness training requires us to examine and adjust our lifestyle. We need to carefully tend the foundational virtues—personal Bible reading and study are essential. Prayer is absolutely important. These activities require time, at least an hour a day, usually more. Attending public worship is important, and those in a godliness training program will not want to miss opportunities for communal Bible study and prayer.

Along with developing these foundational virtues, godliness involves godly acts. Husbands must help and care for their wives; wives must do the same for their husbands. Loving, considerate care of children is part of this picture too. Godliness also requires us to perform our work with excellence. It involves honesty in our business.

Godliness is a big package. It is a quality found in the lives of those who are spiritually fit, just as athletic prowess is found among those who are physically fit. Training for godliness, the apostle says, has value for forever. Physical fitness does not; physically fit bodies ultimately die. The word *godliness* refers to a way of life that we will experience in the life to come, though then it will be elevated many, many times. As it brings us closer to God and provides us with the spiritual power that God supplies, godliness anticipates the way we will be when we are in glory.

The equation looks like this: T4G = T4H. Training for godliness equals training for heaven. That's as good as it gets.

Lord Jesus, you were an athlete who never flinched as you walked
steadfastly toward the cross. Help me today to be focused and diligent
as I train for godliness. I cannot do this without your Holy Spirit.
Come, Holy Spirit, for Jesus' sake, Amen.

FIFTY-TWO

The Circle

*"If anyone chooses to do God's will, he will find out whether
my teaching comes from God or whether I speak on my own."*
—John 7:17

Those who view their lives in the light of eternity deal with a problem that never goes away as long as they live. Why is it that they are so sure about the message of Jesus while many others reject it?

Most people seem to want to go their own way. The last thing they want to hear is that God is displeased with them, and they become extremely irate if anyone suggests that because they reject God's will, they will perish everlastingly.

As we seek to live as forever people whose thoughts and actions are governed by our knowledge of an eternally glorious future, it is important that we understand why so many reject Jesus. It is because of the mysterious circle that Jesus described when he taught at the Feast of the Tabernacles in Jerusalem.

Exactly what it was about his teaching that astonished the Jews who listened to him, we do not know. Very likely, he called people to repentance and announced that the kingdom of heaven was at hand. Whatever it was, those who listened were astonished because Jesus did not have a teaching certificate. He came from a despised region, and there was no record of him ever studying with an illustrious rabbi. Yet he brought teachings that completely overturned their ideas. He healed people on the Sabbath, he called God his Father, and he called the religious leaders "sons of the devil." They were very, very upset.

Jesus then revealed the circle that has to be in place before a person can understand Jesus' teaching. First, there has to be an inner desire to do the will of God. "If anyone chooses to do God's will, he will find out whether my teaching comes from God. . . . "

110

Those who trust in Christ and are trying to do his will should realize that the people around them who reject Christ are doing so because they have not chosen to do God's will. Those who choose their own will or the will of others who oppose Christ, will simply not be able to recognize the truth that Christ has come to bring.

There is a mystery about belief and unbelief. Why do some who hear the Word of Jesus believe that Word and obey it, while others do not? When the gospel is proclaimed, or when individual believers witness to the truth of Christ to a friend or coworker, they can never know if that person is going to respond in faith. That will happen only if he or she has a desire to do God's will. If there is no such desire, the truth of God will go in one ear and out the other.

The apostle Paul says something very similar: "The man without the Spirit does not accept the things that come from the Spirit of God, for they are foolishness to him, and he cannot understand them . . . " (1 Cor. 2:14). When we connect this statement with what Jesus said, we conclude that before people can believe what Jesus says, the Holy Spirit has to equip them to hear and understand. And part of that equipping is that they will want to do the will of God.

This means that when the biblical message comes to people who are disobedient to God, they simply will not be touched by what they hear. It will go right over them or past them. Once people become locked into the disobedient mode, they become virtually dead to the good news of salvation.

As we try to live for Christ, we often become discouraged because other people look askance at us, as if something is wrong. We cannot escape the question "Why am I so sure of what Christ teaches while many of the people I know aren't the least bit interested?" Why? It's because of disobedience.

The flip side is this: our own knowledge of Christ's will for us is directly related to our obedience. If we drift away from the way he wants us to live, we will find that his voice grows ever fainter. Other voices intrude. But as we, who have Christ's Spirit, live in obedience to him, we find our lives enriched immeasurably as Christ's teaching takes deeper root in our hearts.

Holy Spirit, we pray for those who cannot know your will because their sinfulness obscures your words. Break down such barriers and bring change. And make us obedient, so that the rich fullness of your will may influence us each moment. In Christ, Amen.

FIFTY-THREE

Hating This Life

The man who hates his life in this world will keep it for eternal life.
—John 12:25

The word *love* is ambiguous. It can mean many things—some sordid, some sublime. The word *hate* is not. We all know what it means. Christ's words in the passage above would be a lot easier to handle if *hate* had shades of meaning. It does not.

"I hate Michele."

"Johnny, you shouldn't say that. You may say that you don't like what she does to you. You may say that you prefer to be with someone else, but you shouldn't say *hate.*"

Parents may say something like this to their children. But Jesus tells us we should hate our lives in this world. So how can we deal with this?

First of all, we need to remember who said it, and when. The person who said this was both God and man. As God, he knew everything that had caused the misery that had befallen God's good creation. Just how much of this knowledge was at the forefront of his consciousness during his life in the flesh, we do not know. But there is reason to believe that at this point, only days before his crucifixion, his so-called "Messianic consciousness" was at its peak.

Think, for example, of the way God reacted to the horror he observed just before the flood, when the world was full of violence, so evil and so gross that God could do nothing but destroy every creature that breathed. The second person of the Trinity was there when that happened. That's who is saying this.

Remember too that when Jesus spoke those words, he was about to endure the ultimate human rejection of divinity. God created us in his own image so that he could have communion with us, but Jesus knew that the very opposite was about to occur. God's creation was about to reject the Creator.

Jesus spoke as he did about hating our lives in this world because of a vision he had, a vision that none of us, with our cataracts of sinfulness, are able to see very clearly. He had something in view that had not yet been fully established. Jesus did not say that we should hate our lives in this world, and that is that—instead, he said it in a conversation that had glory in view. In spite of the fact that he was about to endure the ultimate indignity of crucifixion, he knew that his upcoming death would bring about his glory. Rather than making a final grim statement, Jesus was speaking about this hate as a way of preserving our lives for something infinitely more fine and wonderful. The person who hates life in this world "will keep it for eternal life."

So we need to see Jesus' words in terms of his unique vision of what this world really is and what is in store for those who serve him. "Whoever serves me must follow me; and where I am, my servant also will be. My Father will honor the one who serves me" (v. 26).

How often do we think about this? Hate the world? We are deeply in love with the world. We play the game of life according to the rules the world lays down. Sometimes we drink of the trough with which it satisfies its ordinary swine. We relish certain things that heaven despises. What does God see when he sees us making our foolish way through a world that we have grown to love?

Possibly if we would think more about Jesus' words, and if we would look at the world more as God does, we would have times of loathing. We might experience times of clarity when we would see ourselves and our attachment to the world as God sees it. There would be times when we would sense something of the purity of eternal life, and we would long to go there.

In the end, it comes down to this: People who hate the world want nothing more than to serve Christ. "Whoever serves me, must follow me. . . . "

Lovers of the world, hear the words of Christ. Turn from that which has you in its thrall and serve this King. If you do, you will discover why Jesus said what he did.

Lord Jesus Christ, thank you for speaking to us with words we cannot misunderstand. Give us a vision that comes close to your vision. Show us what serving you means, and equip us to do so. We pray in your name, Amen.

FIFTY-FOUR

Our Own Worst Enemy

Now to him who is able to do immeasurably more than all we ask or imagine . . .
—Ephesians 3:20

What is hindering the full impact of the gospel of God in our lives and in our families and in our communities and in our nations? Is it the terrifying power of the opposition? Likely not. The reason the Christian community does not more powerfully reflect the power of God is in us. We fail to begin to live up to our potential. We are our own worst enemy.

We are too easily satisfied. Believers tend to congregate in clumps where we create a way of life that becomes mutually acceptable. We soon become satisfied with our level of spiritual experience. We want to be good, but not too good. We want to be Christian enough to make ourselves feel comfortable. We don't realize that if we are truly believers, God has invaded our lives with a power that is immeasurable. We could do so much more. We could be so much more. And our churches could do so much more and be so much more too.

Ephesians 3:20-21 gives us a description of God that is really not surprising: God is the one who is "able to do immeasurably more than all we ask or imagine." We know that; we knew it. After all, God created all things and still controls all things. That's not the surprise here. What is surprising here is that this great power of the true God is located among and connected to believers.

Almighty God has touched our lives. He is "able to do immeasurably more than all we ask or imagine, *according to his power that is at work within us.*" Then this remarkable statement goes on to praise him *in the church* and in Christ Jesus.

This doxology should startle us. The very idea that the immeasurable power of God is not merely diffused through the universe but is centered in the church is so

114

invigorating that it should shatter the complacency of every group of believers who are part of the great church universal. It should shatter the complacency that we have by nature as Christian believers.

A church may never be satisfied with the level it has reached as a church. There is so much we can do and we must do. We may never be satisfied with the level we have reached in our own spiritual life. The Bible is overflowing with announcements that once we are in Christ, we are a new creation, new creatures. It is sinful to continue to describe ourselves in terms of what we are by nature; we must describe ourselves in terms of what God can and will do in us if we totally surrender ourselves to God.

And it is wrong for a group of Christians to say, Oh, we cannot be any different from what we are because we are Dutch you see, or German, or Swedish, or Italian, or African American, or Hispanic, or whatever. Christians cannot and may not talk this way. We have the Spirit of the living God in our hearts, the God who is able to do immeasurably more than we ask or imagine.

How can we change? When we read the marvelous doxology in Ephesians 3, we discover that it directly follows a prayer. The apostle says, "O God, I want your people to grasp how wide and long and high and deep the love of Jesus is. O God, I want your people to know this love that goes far beyond our ability to know. O God, I want them to be filled with the fullness of yourself."

Christians don't transcend the patterns of behavior that make them so satisfied and complacent by hiring a worship consultant and a mission consultant. They do that when they focus their attention on the Lord Jesus Christ. They do that when they stand at the cross and marvel at the fullness of God's holy love that freed them from their sins. They do that when they cheer on resurrection morning, because they know that the dragon has been beaten, and he's tumbling down the hill to hell. They do that when they marvel at the fire and the thunder of Pentecost and understand that the Holy Spirit has come to live in them as individuals and in them together within the church.

The power of God within us and our churches is the greatest power in the world. We have to change so that we can express this divine power in our lives. We cannot even imagine what God will do through us if we stop limiting ourselves.

O God, will you let us do this? We want to be more courageous than we are, more committed than we are, more effective than we are. We are ashamed of our feeble expectations of ourselves. Forgive us. Help us to know the fullness of your love in Christ, and fill us with your Spirit. Amen.

FIFTY-FIVE

Our Lust, Our Pride

*The world and its desires pass away, but the man
who does the will of God lives forever.*
—1 John 2:17

L*ust* is not a nice word—it refers to desires that go beyond the bounds. It refers
to desires that drive us to violate others. It is used often in connection with
sexual drives. Lust corrupts us.

The Bible is candid, and it connects lust with the normal lives of normal people.
We need to drop our guard when we read it. In this case, we discover that *world*
does not mean what we ordinarily associate with worldliness—things like finding
ecstasy at an all-night rave. In 1 John 2:15-17, *world* refers to the lust within us—
lust and pride and boasting.

The world is *in us,* and if we aren't careful, it works itself out.

Everything in the world—the lust of the flesh, the lust of the eyes, and arrogant
boasting—comes not from the Father but from the world. When we realize that the
world is the wanting that our flesh does, we realize why we love it so much. We
have engines inside us that compel us to reach out and look and want with a pas-
sionate wanting of people and things.

It's hard not to love the world when the things for which we lust are alluring and
tantalizing. Some time ago, one of the major advertising corporations installed a bar
in its offices so that creative types could take an alcohol break to make them more
creative; from out of that bar come ideas that make people lust for lots of things.

Those who know that they are God's people who will live forever in Christ's
presence and gladly serve him must find ways to put distance between themselves
and the world. But this is hard to do because, as 1 John 2:15-17 indicates, the

world is inside us. It consists of powerful natural tendencies that are always ready to erupt into controlling forces that drive us to do things we know are wrong.

How can we kill the love of the world within us? Perhaps the first thing we have to do is recognize that old loves die hard. Love is all-consuming, and you don't purge your system of an old love by brushing your teeth.

We also need to understand something that the marketers are doing their best to obscure: What we lust for and the things we are proud of and boast about are passing away. Eighty-five grand will put a Jaguar convertible in your garage, but, little sister, that bright red trophy is passing away, even if you don't drive it in the winter snow.

Same is true of those whose common lusts break up marriages. See the lovers in the dim corner with their drinks, laughing together, both finally sure that they have found someone who truly loves them, someone who truly understands them. Look in on their lives sixteen years later, and see her sallow skin and his vacant stare, and watch them try to make something out of a life that has become awkward and sad.

We have to see with something other than lustful eyes; we have to be smart and intelligent and understand that the world's allure is a sham. It's part of the cosmic con game the world plays with ordinary men and women whose lust never takes a rest.

We don't get rid of our lust by closing our eyes; we kill it by changing our focus. "The world and its desires pass away, but the man who does the will of God lives forever." There it is: it's either/or. Either we will be in sync with everything that is in the world or we will be deeply interested in knowing the will of God and doing it.

Forever people, those who never let the knowledge of their own eternity become obscured by the swirl around them, spend time daily in prayer and with the Holy Scripture. They put themselves in a position of knowing the will of God, and they work at finding ways to obey that will each hour. Their eyes are open, but the lust has gone out of them. They want to see how they can serve the Lord and those around them who need their love and care.

Such people live forever.

Teach us your will, O Lord. All around us are forces and powers that try to turn us aside from your will. But our biggest problem is what's inside us. Smother our natural pride and lust. Help us focus on knowing your will and doing it. Amen.

FIFTY-SIX

Affluenza

Though your riches increase, do not set your heart on them.
—Psalm 62:10

When the history of this era is written, historians will note the outbreak of a new disease—affluenza.

Never before have so many people had so much money. Millions who never expected to be affluent, are. Some of them literally don't know what to do with their money. In one modest California town, one man managed to make enemies of his neighbors and a laughingstock of himself by building a 27,000-square-foot "home" modeled after the palace in Versailles, France. Those who live "next door" to this monstrosity are as mad as hoot owls.

But what do you do when you have more money than you know what to do with? You can build a big house, but you can only live in so many rooms. You can only eat so much food. You can only wear so many clothes. You can only go on so many vacations.

So what do you do when you don't know what to do with your money? How do you avoid affluenza? To start with, you had better read the Bible a lot, and you had better believe it.

Most of us would agree that it's good to be affluent, at least it's better to be affluent than to be poor. Yes, that's true. But it's also extremely dangerous. Attaching the name *affluenza* to this state is not as far-fetched as it may seem. Affluence is dangerous because money is a force with a power beyond reckoning. And the disease that it creates in many affluent people creeps up so subtly that before you can say "Alan Greenspan," the disease has spread through the person's entire system and is incurable.

The New Testament has some pointed remarks about the love of money, which it calls the root of all kinds of evil. Some have pointed out that riches were not considered as much of a problem in the Old Testament because God seemed to show favor to his people by giving them lots of cattle and fabulous harvests. But that's not really true. Psalm 62 says that we should not set our hearts on riches when they increase.

And if affluent people are looking for a vaccination to protect them from affluenza, they can do no better than read Psalm 49 every other week or so. That psalm is very realistic about riches. It concludes with a real downer: "A man who has riches without understanding is like the beasts that perish."

"Understanding" apparently is the key to immunity when it comes affluenza. We have to understand a few things if we are going to handle our wealth properly. Today's verse from Psalm 62, along with just about all of Psalm 49, can help us develop that understanding.

Point number one made by Psalm 49 is this: if you are going to handle your wealth properly, you have to remember at all times that affluence is temporary. Relentlessly the psalm hammers home the point: you cannot hold on to your wealth tight enough to insure that you will never have to give it up. Ultimately the affluent will leave their wealth to others. The poetry of Psalm 49 would be beautifully moving if it were not talking about such a ghastly subject. But notice this description of rich people: "Like sheep they are destined for the grave, and death will feed on them. . . . Their forms will decay in the grave, far from their princely mansions" (v. 14). "Far from their princely mansions"—never forget that phrase.

Point number two: remember that no matter how rich you become, you will never have enough money to buy what you need the most. Never. Here it is: "No man can redeem the life of another or give to God a ransom for him—the ransom for a life is costly, no payment is ever enough—that he should live on forever and not see decay" (vv. 7-8).

My soul needs to be redeemed. I need to be saved from hell. I can never do that, no matter how rich I become. God alone does that. It takes blood, God's blood, to save people. And that blood is so infinitely valuable, it makes whatever we have look like sawdust. We just have to trust Christ. We have to run as fast as we can to him and ask him to be our Savior. He will put everything into perspective for us. He can make sick people well, even those who have affluenza.

O God, how puny we are, even with all our wealth. You are so great and merciful. Give us understanding, and humble us. Help us realize how much we need someone to pay for our soul. May we flee to Jesus, your Son, who, though he was rich, for our sakes became poor so that we, through his poverty, might have true riches. In his name, Amen.

FIFTY-SEVEN

Laying Up Treasure

*They will lay up treasure for themselves as a firm
foundation for the coming age. . . .*
—1 Timothy 6:19

If there is anything in the Bible that confirms that human nature has not changed, it's the statements about the way money can lay hold on people. One of these is found at the end of Paul's first letter to Timothy, where he indicates that there were people in the Ephesian church who had money, and their money had them in a vice grip.

Some of them, apparently, had found a way to profit financially from their religious activities. The apostle writes about those who have been "robbed of the truth and who think that godliness is a means of financial gain."

The same perverse thinking exists today—large empires are built on religion. They may have been started with the best of intentions, but somewhere along the line the religious program turned into a business. Nothing corrupts religion faster than money. And nothing corrupts us more than money. "People who want to get rich fall into temptation and a trap and into many foolish and harmful desires that plunge men into ruin and destruction" (1 Tim. 6:9).

But it doesn't have to be that way. Rich people can pray for God's special grace that helps them use their money properly. Paul tells Timothy how to deal with money lovers. The alternative to money love is to love the kind of life that lasts and lasts and lasts . . . forever.

The Bible tells those who are in love with money (as most of us are, to some extent) to think sensibly. First Timothy 6:19 contrasts the accumulation of material wealth to the accumulation of real wealth. Earthly wealth is an illusion. Money is a mocker, like wine. It makes people look silly. One day they think they are rich, the next day they can be down in the dumps because they have lost some of their precious money.

Those who are rich must stop chasing after something that is as fragile as a spider web. Rich people should be "rich in good deeds and willing to share," and then they will (notice this carefully!) "lay up treasure for themselves as a firm foundation for the coming age, so that they may take hold of the life that is truly life."

If a person with millions of dollars of venture capital can become excited because of a business deal that promises to give a great return on the dollar, how much more excited should all of us be about the equation the Bible sets up here? It looks like this: Don't love money, but use it to do good deeds; then you will lay up treasures for yourselves that will be a foundation for the coming age, and you will be able to take hold of that which is truly life.

Now, with a deal like that, it doesn't take a lot of investment intelligence to understand how to live. I have to monitor my own life closely to make sure that I am not doing what I do for money. You have to do the same. To be sure, we need to be frugal, wise, and diligent so that we will have what we need for our families and for our own care. But when we have more money available than we need, something inside of us becomes attached to money itself.

We want the sense of power that goes along with money. We want the nice things that money can buy. We want the pleasures that money can buy. We want money itself. We just like to see it accumulate and grow. And as it does, we become more and more attached to it.

This is madness. Of course those who do not know the Bible and Jesus Christ as their Lord cannot be expected to realize how insane money love is. That is all they have. But when someone who has been saved by Christ and filled with his Spirit is in love with money, we need to put our arm over his or her shoulder and softly say, "Hey, good friend, do you realize you are making the worst possible investment? Why not invest in life that never ends?"

It is astonishing that we can lay up treasures in heaven while we are in this world. Here's one investment that seems too good to be true, but it really is true. God says: "Don't think about money. Get a life that is really life, life that will last forever."

O Lord God, we hear what you are saying, but it's hard to get our minds off money. Please, oh, please help us build a foundation for eternal life. Your Son became poor so that we could become rich, really rich forever. May we never forget that. Amen.

FIFTY-EIGHT

Acting Like a Kid

*I press on toward the goal to win the prize for which
God has called me heavenward in Christ Jesus.*
—Philippians 3:14

O bviously, the apostle Paul was writing figuratively here: he could no more actually do what he describes here than a turtle could best a rabbit across my backyard. There wasn't any room in his prison cell to run, and the truth is, his knees weren't that great anymore. But here he writes about himself as if he were an Olympic marathoner rounding the last turn in the road by the aqueduct, heading for the finish line.

In order to understand the significance of his outburst, we need to realize just how absurd this figure of speech actually is. What was Paul's problem? Was he hallucinating? Did he think he was a kid again?

To start out with, he was in prison. Doing time. Moreover, he was getting on in years; it was time for him to settle back and become a sort of elder statesman. His circumstances simply did not support this kind of fierce dedication in the service of the Lord.

But on a deeper level, there are many reasons to figure that Paul, of all people, should be somewhat more content. After all, he wasn't a kid doing cross-country in high school. He had already made an enormous contribution to the work of Christ and the expansion of the church. As he did his time, he could tick off in his mind while praying the churches he had founded: Ephesus, Colosse, Derbe, Lystra, Thessalonica, and lots of other places, among them Philippi, to which he wrote these words. Time to cut back, Paul, turn things over to others and relax, not talk about forgetting all these years of service and acting as if you're just starting in the service of Christ.

Perhaps the main reason Paul shouldn't be writing about himself this way is that he was a Calvinist. He was the one who furnished the church with heavy doctrinal material we have to read three times to catch, and when we come back to it three months later, we have to start at ground zero. Paul was the man who talked about the predestinating will of God and about the way God controls everything. As he put it once: "For from him and through him and to him are all things" (Rom. 11:36). Where did he think he fit into all this?

There have been many cases of people who have concluded from Paul's teachings that we don't have much to do when it comes to working for Jesus. Such people are missing the connection between Paul's teaching and the Lord Jesus Christ. When believers take Paul's teachings and turn them into a manual that describes the way things are supposed to work, without connecting everything to Jesus Christ, they can easily become spectators instead of marathoners.

What was it that made Paul think of himself as a runner, lungs bursting, totally focused on the goal? Let's call it the "goal prize." This magnificent athlete for Christ realized that there was more besides what he already knew and experienced. That "moreness" was connected in every way with Christ himself. A few sentences before he described himself as an Olympic athlete, Paul wrote: "I want to know Christ and the power of his resurrection . . . " (v. 10).

Doctrine he gave us, and surpassing accomplishment in God's mission, but this man never forgot that Christ was always to be the center of his attention and that the Christian faith is about power. It is the very power of Christ's resurrection that flows into the lives of believers; it is that power that equips them to do great things for God and to act like kids, even when we would never expect them to act that way.

It is closeness to Christ and the fullness of his power that enables elderly prisoners to exert themselves in the service of Christ. It is the daily recurring experience of Christ's glorious restoration that empowers those who praise God for his sovereign grace to run beside God as he executes his glorious plan.

There's something here for all of us, maybe especially for elderly Calvinists who need to be encouraged to run like kids as they serve their Savior. People who have been overwhelmed by the same "heavenly calling" Paul experienced want the power of Christ's resurrection to flow through them.

Risen Lord Jesus Christ, help us to yearn for and reach for a greater experience of your nearness and your power in us. Help us forget past sins and triumphs and stretch out toward the goal that you have revealed in your Word. Forgive us for being less enthusiastic than we should be. In your mercy hear us. Amen.

FIFTY-NINE

The Grand Cherokee

Establish the work of our hands.
—Psalm 90:17

If you are looking to buy a Jeep Grand Cherokee sometime during 2001, there's a good chance it will have an interior upgrade. The panels along the lower edge of the doors that look like real wood aren't real wood as I write this, but Daimler Chrysler intends to make them real wood sometime during 2001. Like the trim on a Mercedes—that's real wood already. Actually, the company wanted the real wood earlier, but when you are producing several hundred thousand units, you can't just snap your fingers and make it happen. Ask Mike about that.

He's an engineer with the company that makes many of the components of the Grand Cherokee interior, and he has been working on this change for several months already. There's a lot of engineering that goes into creating each real wood panel and making sure that it's attached properly. It should be all taken care of by next year . . . but it could take even longer.

When I talked with Mike about this, the thought struck me that Mike and his colleagues are spending a lot of time and energy on something that is not really very significant in the great scheme of things. What difference does it actually make if the Grand Cherokee has real wood along the bottom of its doors or it doesn't? The wood trim on the doors will have absolutely no effect on the performance of the vehicle, none whatsoever. Ultimately every one of these grand vehicles will end up in the great cosmic junkyard. Mike is wasting his time. Mike is wasting his life.

But just a minute. We can make the same observation about all sorts of activities that many of us spend our entire lives doing. Take engineers. For every single item we use there were engineers to figure out how to produce it and to make sure it would operate as expected. Some products—like scalpels and toothbrushes—are absolutely necessary, but others—like decorative design features in cars—are of no actual use whatsoever.

Say you're a Christian. Are you wasting your life if you spend it at work that has no abiding value? Not necessarily. Let's get back to Mike. When we talked, we were both celebrating the completion of the Christian school his children attend. Obviously, he was being paid for getting the wood panel in place in the Grand Cherokee, paid fairly well in fact. And he was using his income to provide for the ordinary needs of his wife and children and to support his church and to make sure that his children would be educated at a school in which all the learning is done in the light of the Bible.

The school his children attend is not Christian merely because some devotional exercises occur in it. It provides a Christian education that is dedicated to enabling children to understand that they should see everything in their lives in the light of God's Word. Proverbs 1:7—"The fear of the Lord is the beginning of knowledge"—plays an important role in the school's understanding of education.

The very evening we talked, we heard the children of the school express the grand philosophy of education that makes the school Christian. They sang about the difference between building on the rock that is Jesus Christ and building on the sand. The teachers in that school never let the children forget that they are learning about God's creation, not something that came into existence by chance. They never let them forget either that they are living in a fallen world in which there are absolute principles of right and wrong. They also teach them that they are God's children and that the resources of God's Holy Spirit are there for them to use as they serve him.

This school is Mike's school. As Mike and his fellow Christian friends work to make that school possible, they are building the kingdom of God. As he uses what he earns to serve Christ in his home, in his church, and in his children's school, he transforms what Daimler Chrysler wants for the Grand Cherokee into something that has eternal value. Every Grand Cherokee is going to disappear, whether it has real wood trim on its doors or not, but the kingdom of Christ will endure forever.

Could it be that Moses had something like all this in mind when he asked God to establish the work of his hands?

Christ Jesus, it would be nice if everything we did could have lasting significance and meaning, but it just doesn't work out that way for us while we are here. Make us willing to use the fruits of our ordinary labor to do extraordinary things. We want to seek your kingdom first of all. Help us do that. Amen.

SIXTY

Ko Pha-Ngan

God gave them over to sinful desires of their hearts to
sexual impurity for the degrading of their bodies. . . .
—Romans 1:24

Sometimes those who have lived among God's covenant people for a long time become restless, even bored. The Christian way is a good and wholesome way, but there are those living among the forever people who think that it might be exciting to venture outside the circle of grace once in awhile and see what's going on.

It's important to realize that what's out there is pretty horrible actually. For example, look what's happening on the island of Ko Pha-Ngan in the Gulf of Thailand, just off the coast of Thailand. On the white sugar sand of Hat Rin Beach, young people from Europe and America plunge deep into hedonistic decadence.

Time magazine described the depths of debauchery that have taken over this colony of young people. A local police captain is quoted as saying, "What they seem to be doing is smoking a lot of dope, having sex with each other, and walking around in their underwear." But that's not the half of it. The full moon all-night raves on the beach recreate the depths of paganism, the very paganism that existed when the Bible was written.

Movie idol Leonardo DeCaprio starred in *The Beach,* a film that lionized what's happening on Ko Pha-Ngan island, and a lot of young people have seen it. Those who chafe at the bit while they live among the people of God sometimes conclude that life would be more exciting somewhere else—outside the place of grace.

We must all remember, and we must find a way to tell our young people, that the people of God have an alternative to what happens among those who reject God and go their own way. The orgiastic debauchery at full moon on Hat Rin

Beach is as old as sin, and the Holy Spirit created the Bible so that God's people could be delivered from such ruin.

Those dear, pitiable young people who are destroying themselves in Thailand are just one example out of millions who are doing the same throughout the world, and who have been doing this for centuries. The nations that surrounded Israel were so corrupted by their depravity that the Lord arranged to have them destroyed. And in the New Testament era, the apostle Paul referred more than once to what he saw as he trudged through the empire. His description in Romans 1:24-32 causes us to shudder as we not only sense its horror but recognize that the apostle is talking about circumstances that are duplicated now.

In Ephesians 2:3, Paul describes the paganism the first Christians had been rescued from: "All of us also lived among them at one time, gratifying the cravings of our sinful nature and following its desires and thoughts. Like the rest, we were by nature objects of wrath."

Those who live where the Word of God is obeyed and the holy sacraments bring grace, where believers speak in psalms, hymns, and spiritual songs, and where there are occasions to exult over evidence of God's healing mercy, can easily become oblivious to the moral depravity around them. It is dangerous to let this happen. We must not drop our guard, we must not fail to fortify one another and especially our children, who breathe the vapors of this degenerate age.

To keep alert, we do not need Leonardo DiCaprio, nor even *Time* magazine and other media who delight in titillating their viewers and readers with tales from the Gulf of Thailand. We need only the Bible. This realistic book depicts not only the degradation of the nations surrounding Israel and the early church but also the stumbling and the failures of the covenant people of God—even of their leaders.

Hat Rin Beach is not half a world away—it is within everyone. The cruel sensuality found on its moonlit sand resonates within our hearts. We must be vigilant and smart. We must keep telling one another, "No, that is not the way to live. That is the way of death. The way of life is the way of the Bible, the way of Christ, the way of the Spirit of the Lord."

Pity the poor children who dance on the edge of hell when the moon is full on Hat Rin Beach. If we hold fast to the alternative way of life the Lord has given us, we and our children will be able to help them.

O God, as we see the power of sin, we beseech you to hold us fast in your purifying love. Help us resist such evil in our own lives, and use us to display a better way to those who are part of that destructive scene. May many of them come and join us. In Christ, Amen.

SIXTY-ONE

Instead of Futility

You must no longer live as the Gentiles do, in the futility of their thinking. . . .
—Ephesians 4:17

I f we are going to live with the sense that we will live forever, it is necessary for us to think clearly. The Gentiles, to whom the apostle refers in Ephesians 4, were besotted and dissolute because their thinking had become hopelessly entangled with destructive ideas.

We should not think of these Gentiles as particularly vicious people who stalked through the land, intent on destroying God's truth. As it turns out, most of them were very ordinary people, nice enough on the outside. But when we probe beneath the surface and get to know them, we discover just how futile their minds had become.

There are five young women living together in campus housing at a northwestern college who exhibit this same futility, though you would not consider them especially evil if you were to meet them. They are a studious bunch who spend most of their time during the week studying. Correspondence that I received from one of them mentioned that they usually have the television on. She also said that there was a lot of drinking on weekends. And since there was a lot of pot around their campus, there was a lot of pot smoking too, though, she assured me, everything was actually pretty tame.

She was responding to something I had written about the movie *Mission to Mars,* which suggested that life on earth came into existence when a spaceship from Mars landed here with a family of humanoids from the green planet. That happened three and a half billion years ago; and, in case you are wondering where we came from, there's your answer. The young woman who wrote me from that dorm room thought that it was one plausible idea among several others she considered plausible as well.

She then favored me with her own feelings regarding the beginning of life on earth. She said she figured that it happened pretty much the way they taught it in the schools. The process went something like this: Water gave birth to life, which gradually evolved, became conscious, and voila—here we are. But, she conceded, it is impossible to know for sure how it all started.

Her theory of origins struck me as somewhat unique; I had never encountered anything quite so simple. I wonder whether the idea that life came from water is really being taught in the schools. The details, however, are not all that important. What is important about this scenario is that we have campus housing in which young women live who study hard all week, drink on weekends and smoke a little pot, and figure that everything around them came from some unknown and unknowable process that most likely started with water.

These young women are not particularly vicious either, though if we were to study their behavior, we might be shocked by some of it. They are among the cream of the crop of American college students actually, and they are simply being what American public education, American homes, and the American culture makes people. They are prisoners of futile thinking. It will take a miracle of the Holy Spirit, literally, to change them.

The only way believers today can live with the assurance that they have a carefully laid-out eternal future is by knowing that God carefully controlled everything that has brought us to this point. We need to know that God is the creator of this earth and the entire universe, and that every process within it is under God's control. If it were true that there are areas of reality that God has nothing to do with, then God would actually be as much a victim of circumstances as we would be.

The biblical teaching regarding origins is the foundation for everything else in the Bible. Not only is God revealed as the one who made the heavens and the earth, but the Son of God, Jesus Christ, is presented as the person through whom all things have been made. Those who view the idea of creation as quaint and unworthy of serious attention, and who consider any theory of origins plausible, are doomed to futility as they try to figure out their lives and live meaningfully.

We must do all we can to insure that our children will not have their heads filled with nonsense when they think about the beginnings of life and the beginning of our race. Whether or not we have an eternal future depends on whether or not we know who created us and who controls the past.

Merciful God, we pray for these college girls. And we pray too for this nation that provides its youth with such a flimsy and futile view of origins. Thank you for the Scriptures that tell us the truth about our beginnings and assure us of a glorious future. In Christ's name, Amen.

SIXTY-TWO

"Holy, Holy, Holy!"

"Holy, holy, holy is the LORD Almighty; the whole earth is full of his glory."
—Isaiah 6:3

If you are looking for something to calm you down, lower your blood pressure, and take away the anxiety that makes your chest tight, sit down, throw your head back, stretch out, and think about the holiness of God.

One of the reasons we are harried and tense is that we don't think about God enough, and we think about ourselves too much. When we do think about God, we often feel a little bit rebellious or we have big questions that vex us—Why, God, are you doing this to me? Why is this happening?

The message about God that dominates everything else is that God is holy. When Jesus' disciples asked him to teach them to pray, the first thing he said we should pray is for God's name to be made holy—hallowed. That means we should pray that people like us think about him as a holy God and praise him as a holy God.

One of the problems we have when we read the Bible is that suddenly we come upon something so astonishing it is mind-boggling, but it doesn't look any different on the printed page. There are no blazing colors painted around those sentences—they look like all the others. But when we read them, we should sit bolt upright and say Wow!

The opening of Isaiah 6 is one such passage. The prophet announces that he "saw the Lord, seated on a throne, high and exalted. . . . " Above his head there were six glorious angels, called seraphs, who were calling to one another, "Holy, holy, holy is the LORD Almighty, the whole earth is full of his glory."

God is holy. Think of how often people say other things are holy—things like cows, like Toledo, and smoke, and even cats. What gross profanity! God alone is holy. God alone is holy. God alone is holy. He is. Through and through, totally, always, eternally holy.

What does this mean? That everything God plans, thinks, and does is righteous and just and good. God is separated totally from sin; sin does not corrupt God's actions nor contaminate his being. Everything God has done in connection with the creation of the world, everything God does as he controls history, everything he does in our lives, and everything he ever will do is perfect.

For Isaiah, the sheer holiness of God appeared as God presented himself to the stricken prophet in all the glory of his majesty. God's holiness and his glory are virtually the same; he has a glorious holiness and a holy glory.

We must think about this more often. More often? Every day we must think of this. As we begin our day in quiet prayer before God, it is good to compose our hearts, simply remembering that the God whom we address in prayer is holy. It is good, in the quiet of the early morning, to remember again that God is in total control of every event in our lives, and that God will work out his plan in terms of his holiness.

The whole earth is full of God's glory. We must learn to see this even when we face upsetting and unpleasant things in our own lives. When we begin each day by remembering that God always does exactly what is right, we may be sure that what occurs in our lives will somehow express his perfection.

And when we think about God's holiness and the glory that radiates from it, it humbles us and lets us see who we really are and where we really belong. We are not God. We may not question what God does in our lives. We must simply trust him. And we must ask God to forgive us for forgetting his holiness as much as we do. We must ask him to forgive us for being so unholy ourselves.

Isaiah staggered from God's throne room crying, "Woe to me! I am ruined! For I am a man of unclean lips, and I live among a people of unclean lips, and my eyes have seen the King, the LORD Almighty" (v. 5).

What more can we say? Let us think about our holy and glorious God, and let us feel the overwhelming joy that comes from knowing that we will see the seraphim someday ourselves. And more than likely, we will join the choir that never stops singing, "Holy, holy, holy is the LORD Almighty; the whole earth is full of his glory."

O Lord, forgive me for not thinking about your holiness more than I do. Thank you for letting me catch a glimpse into heaven, where I can see for a split second how gloriously holy you are. Forgive my sin that makes me unholy. Help me rest in you and trust you again today, O blessed God. In Christ, Amen.

SIXTY-THREE

The Meaning of Love

This is how we know what love is: Jesus Christ laid down his life for us.
—1 John 3:16

Look around at what is happening these days, and you'll find much that is hideous. Pornography is. Abortion is. Divorce is. The abuse of children is. The corruption of language is.

The corruption of language? Hideous? Isn't that a little strong?

Not really. Especially when we think of the way perfectly good words are pre-empted by those who have no right to use them. Take the word *gay*, for example. Fifty years ago, it described happy people and circumstances. Dickens used it a lot; translations of Tolstoy use it a lot. Today, it means the very opposite of what it used to mean. Are gays gay?

The word *love* has been corrupted too. Think of what it means these days. In some cases, possibly most, it refers only to sex. The other day I was embarrassed when Rodale (the people who publish *Prevention* magazine) sent me a letter with the following written across the top: "This is only for people 18 and above who have had sexual experience." There were other provocative statements and photos on the outside of the envelope. On the same day they sent a book that was sup-posed to help people find natural remedies for their ailments. I refused them both, and sent them a letter expressing my outrage. This is what love has become for many people most of the time.

When we turn from the hideous corruption of human language that poisons the mind and paralyzes thought, and turn instead to the Bible for the meaning of love, we are forced to reset our minds. Love is precisely defined: "This is love: not that we loved God, but that he loved us and sent his Son as an atoning sacrifice for our sins" (1 John 4:10).

Christian believers must always think of Christ and his sacrifice when they think of love. "This is how we know what love is: Jesus Christ laid down his life for us. And we ought to lay down our lives for our brothers" (1 John 3:16). It's the exact opposite of what love means in everyday language. Common ideas about love relate to satisfying our deepest longings. We love chocolate cake because it satisfies a craving we have for chocolate and sugar. Gentlemen prefer blondes because they satisfy some kind of craving within them. And lots of people who are deeply in love with someone would have to admit that their love is nothing but a selfish passion they have for that person. They want to possess that person. They want that person to satisfy them.

This is not what the Bible has in mind when it says, for example: "And this is [God's] command: to believe in the name of his Son, Jesus Christ, and to love one another as he commanded us" (1 John 3:23). When God calls us to love one another, he is calling us to live sacrificially for each other.

This is true of the love between a man and a woman in marriage. The intimate relationship a husband and wife have with one another is designed to be something like the love Christ has for his church. True, in marriage there are high moments where partners satisfy one another's sexual needs, but these are only part of a very large and complex picture. The intimacies of marriage are as wonderful as they are because they arise out of the marriage partners' mutual desire to care for one another. "Husbands, love your wives, just as Christ loved the church and gave himself up for her to make her holy" (Eph. 5:25).

We must love as Christ loved. But not only in marriage. Loving as Christ loved means that we must help people who are in need. "If anyone has material possessions and sees his brother in need but has no pity on him, how can the love of God be in him?" (1 John 3:17). Good question.

When people become Christians they receive a new vocabulary. Love means sacrifice. It means being like Jesus. Not only in our marriages, but in the church, which must be a place where people are sensitive to one another's needs and where they help those who are needy. The church is a place where words are reclaimed and restored, where people think clearly once again, and where they act as Jesus would act if he were in their place.

Loving Savior, give us a faith that understands what you have done for us when you loved us enough to die for us. Help us not "to love with words or tongue but with actions and in truth." Help us to be willing to love sacrificially, the way you did. Amen.

SIXTY-FOUR

Why We Blow It

All Scripture is God-breathed and is useful for teaching,
rebuking, correcting and training in righteousness.
—2 Timothy 3:16

When we are disappointed with ourselves for failing to be the kind of Christians we ought to be, we often think we would have done a lot better if only we had lived in Antioch in A.D. 40, when the gifts of the Spirit resulted in a church that was full of super-Christians. We share an unspoken assumption that the best Christians lived about 2,000 years ago, so we cannot expect the people of God nowadays to measure up to their performance. We do our best, but what can we really expect of Christians in our time?

Actually, this idea is pretty ridiculous. It is true that during the apostolic time there were many manifestations of the Holy Spirit: Peter presenting Dorcas to her gathered friends after they had washed her body and prepared to put her away for good; the man crippled from birth, dancing next to Peter and John. And Antioch itself was the site of several miracles as well. But think about it. Christians today have more than Christians had then.

Take the Bible, for example. Christians then didn't have the Bible as we have it. I doubt that the apostle Paul ever read the gospel of Matthew, and certainly the Christians in Antioch described in Acts 13:1-3 never had personal Bibles they could read regularly and make notes in. In fact, it's only in the last hundred years or so that the Bible has been circulated widely. All Christians in North America are able to have their own copies. We can attend churches where the Word of God is preached; we have access to all sorts of agencies that help us know the Bible and understand it.

We have everything the early believers had, plus much more. As for the manifestations of the Holy Spirit back then and the miracles—well, we have an inspired record of many of them. They are part of our treasury of miracles as well as theirs. And in addition to the actual events the early Christians witnessed, we have the doctrinal elements in the Bible that examine the meaning of these events. We also have the seasoned counsel of the apostles about how we should live. In establishing the inspiration of the Bible in his letter to Timothy, the apostle Paul did not suggest that Christians should henceforth honor, possibly even worship, this book; instead he emphasized the practical significance of this divine gift. Now we can be instructed and rebuked and corrected and trained in righteousness.

We are superbly well-equipped to be the kind of Christians God wants us to be. If ever there were a time when ordinary believers could be forever people who know that they have come from God and that their experience with God is going to last forever and ever, it is now. Right now. With all the means of grace available to us, we should expect that the people of God today would be the most vigorous, energetic, dedicated believers the world has ever seen.

So what went wrong?

Several things. First of all, we could point to the overpowering worldliness in our environment and admit that we have made compromises with it. Worldliness is another name for idolatry, and to the degree that it establishes a beachhead in our lives, we are out of step with the Holy Spirit. But the main reason individual Christians and the church as a whole don't have a very good record when it comes to living as we should is that we ignore the book. It is there, and it is all we need. It is complete. We know about Moses and about the prophet like Moses—Jesus—and we have the teachings of James and the writings of the apostles. We have an inspired history of what happened at the beginning, during Jesus' ministry, and during the days of the early church. It is all there.

Use it and we will be properly taught, shown the way of righteousness, and corrected. But we pay more attention to Paul Harvey and Walter Bennett and AOL and Sammy Sosa and lots of other people. We are convinced that all of them are very important, and we figure that if we take a peek into the Bible for a few minutes each day, we're doing okay. We couldn't be more mistaken.

Come Holy Spirit, heavenly dove, give us a spirit of repentance,
and teach us to turn with hunger and expectation to your Word.
We don't have any excuse for not being better Christians.
Please forgive us, and help us change. For Jesus' sake, Amen.

SIXTY-FIVE

Reading Ezekiel

"Son of man, can these bones live?" I said, "O Sovereign LORD, you alone know."
—Ezekiel 37:3

What is the mark of those who are forever people bound for eternity in the presence of God? We could give several answers to this question. Here is one possibility: a person who reads the Old Testament book of Ezekiel occasionally and gets something out of it.

For those whose responsibilities include reading the Bible over and over again—preachers are such people—the book of Ezekiel can pose something of a problem. For one thing, it is terribly long, eighty-four pages in my Bible. It is shorter than Isaiah and Jeremiah, but somehow it seems longer. Parts of it are baffling, like the wheels within the wheels and other bizarre visions. Besides, it makes me cringe sometimes. But there it is. It is the Word of God, and it must be read and pondered regularly.

Often, we Christians tell each another that Bible reading is a good thing, giving the impression that it is always a pleasant, inspiring experience. That can be true for those who select what they read carefully. After all, there are beautiful psalms and countless verses that lay a brilliant light across our path. And then there is Ezekiel. Some days getting through a piece of it requires sheer determination.

Chapter 16, for example, is grotesque. Using image after image, Ezekiel tells the story of how the nation of Israel received God's mercy, only to prostitute itself as it pursued its sordid adulteries. Ezekiel's realistic language leaves little to the imagination. When my friend David Feddes wrote about this chapter in the devotional booklet *Today,* my wife and I wondered if it was really necessary for him to call all this embarrassing detail to our attention. Unfortunately, it is necessary. We need to know that the God who saves us, saves us while we are yet sinners, while we are ugly with our stain and our soil.

Yes, it's necessary to read material like this. And when we set our mind to it, we will discover the great message of salvation that cascades from these troubling pages. For all the hideous detail the prophet Ezekiel relentlessly reports, the ultimate message is the message of restoration.

In the 37th chapter, we stand amid a valley filled with dried bones, the pathetic residue of a thoroughly dead nation. Obviously, every human possibility has been exhausted. There is no hope whatsoever for those who lie in that bone yard. But God comes rushing in with the wind of the Holy Spirit, and, as the astonished prophet gazes on the incredible scene, life returns.

David Feddes lifted our hearts with his comments on this miraculous restoration: "Never underestimate God's life-giving power. God takes the bleached bones of a dead nation and raises up a vast army. God takes dead hearts and makes them pound with life. God takes dead churches and brings revival. God takes horrid, hopeless situations and makes them heavenly. God takes a crucified corpse and makes it gloriously alive and immortal. And the risen Christ will take millions who have died and raise them to life in immortal bodies to share in his everlasting kingdom."

As we mature in the Christian faith, and the Holy Spirit opens our hearts to more and more of God's truth and prepares us for eternity, we discover in a book like Ezekiel just how marvelous God's salvation really is. Ezekiel shows us the stupidity and disaster of rebellion against God. He shows us the inevitability of judgment upon our rebellion, and he shows us the divine mercy that finally prevails.

We need to encourage one another to grow in our knowledge of the Bible. We need people to lead us through a book like this, taking us by the hand and helping us understand what is happening. We need churches where the message of the entire Scripture comes across in all its power: Human beings are indescribably sinful, always have been and always will be, but God has prepared for each of us a way of salvation through Jesus Christ as we repent of our sins and flee to him.

I love the way Ezekiel finally ends (and usually, I am relieved)—with the description of a wonderful city. And this is its name: "THE LORD IS THERE." Great city. I want to spend forever within its walls.

Sovereign God, forgive us for not always being able to handle the fullness of your Word. Thank you for giving us so much to think about; now, we pray, give us the ability to think deeply about your way with your people throughout the centuries. In Christ's name, Amen.

SIXTY-SIX

Listening Helps

"'Why do you look for the living among the dead?'"
—Luke 24:5

When angels ask questions, we should all pay attention. Among the astonishing events that happened on the morning Jesus rose from the dead, the question two angels asked three excellent women is worth looking at very closely.

We sometimes overlook the fact that all of Jesus' followers who played a role in those events were engaged in activity that was totally unnecessary. At least the angels figured it was. That's why these two, dressed in lightning-bright robes, asked the women point-blank what in the world they were doing at the empty tomb of Jesus with a bag of spices and containers of perfume.

The truth is, these women were caught red-handed. The spices and the perfume they carried were a dead giveaway. Obviously they had not been paying attention to the clear announcement that Jesus had made repeatedly: he was only going to stay in the grave for three days. Jesus had not beat around the bush about either his suffering or his glorious escape from death.

Matthew 16 provides one example among many others in the Bible that the announcement of Jesus' death and resurrection was an ongoing element of his teaching to his disciples. "From that time on Jesus began to explain to his disciples that he must go to Jerusalem and suffer . . . and that he must be killed and on the third day be raised to life" (v. 21). And when Peter, one of Jesus' foremost disciples, displayed a complete lack of comprehension about this, Jesus lambasted him with some of the harshest words he ever addressed to anybody: "Get behind me, Satan! You are a stumbling block to me; you do not have in mind the things of God . . ." (v. 23).

These three women who met the angels that resurrection morning knew about this teaching too; they had accompanied the disciples and Jesus for countless miles of their journeys. But somehow it had sailed over their heads.

In retrospect, this grand missing of the point among Jesus' followers is an embarrassment for all believers. For who among us could ever say that we would not have done the same? Surely, we are no better than these dear fellow travelers of the Master.

From the perspective of the angels, missing what Jesus had so plainly spoken was incredible. Angels, we may be sure, followed the progress of Jesus' ministry with great care, noting his every word and nuance. We know that to be true of the fallen angels who dogged Jesus' footsteps. And doubtlessly where the demons gathered, the holy angels also hovered, protecting the very God they worshiped. They had sung when he was born, and for them the great bright spot in the hideous pattern of Jesus' humiliation was that, once the cross was history, resurrection day would surely come. They knew that. How had the women missed it? So the angels' question is almost sarcastic—its very structure emphasizes the absurdity of the women's actions. They have come in mourning to a birthday party.

Of course, we are no different from the women and the disciples, no different whatsoever. We do not listen to the Savior when he speaks to us. We read his Word, often with exemplary regularity, but the real meaning of what we read blows over us. And that is why we often look for the living among the dead! This happens among people who don't know Christ. But even followers of Christ seek for life where there is no life to be found. Sometimes, this is expressed in self-indulgence. Even believers can trip over stupid things . . . things like alcohol, like sexual immorality, like greed, like materialism, like relentless striving for achievement. There we stand, caught red-handed, looking for life in a cemetery.

Oh, how we must listen to Christ! Let's be honest: most of the words that wash over our consciousness each day have nothing to do with life that lasts eternally. Earnestly, eagerly, we need to turn away from most of it; we need to sift that which might possibly be valuable. And we must discipline ourselves to pay attention to what Christ said.

That, and that alone, will keep us from doing dumb things like seeking the living among the dead.

Living Christ, give us your Spirit so that we can listen to what you are saying to us. Just now, we hear you telling us that one of these days, possibly soon and very soon, you are coming back. Help us to get ready for that. In your name, Amen.

SIXTY-SEVEN

Heaven Is Not Just for Music Majors

Fill the earth and subdue it.
—Genesis 1:28

I can understand why lots of people are not all that interested in dying and going to heaven. I'm talking about Christians—there are Christians who would gladly arrange to stay here forever if they could get away with it. From what they know, heaven will be a great place for music majors, but they are not all that interested in music. They expect to be extremely bored.

I would feel the same way if I were told that heaven is going to be an endless round of golf. Not just nine holes, not just eighteen, not even just thirty-six, but one million holes to the millionth power, and then another round after that.

It is true that there is going to be glorious music in heaven, and we will join the angels in singing God's praises eternally (Rev. 5:11-14). But that's not the whole story. In order to find out what heaven is going to be like, we need to go to the first chapter of the Bible. There we learn that after God created humanity in his own image, he gave Adam and Eve a job to do. "Fill the earth and subdue it," God said. And they set about doing exactly that.

Singing is fine, but we should understand that being created in the image of God means that we were created to work. Work is glorious; it's actually heavenly. Once we are in the presence of God, we are going to be engaged in satisfying, rewarding, and fulfilling work forever (and we won't get tired of it).

We are the imagebearers of God, and we are being renewed to look more and more like him: "[You] have put on the new self, which is being renewed in knowledge in the image of its Creator" (Col. 3:10). Now, the true God who is revealed in the Bible is a worker. Jesus stressed that when he said, "My Father is always at his work to this very day, and I, too, am working" (John 5:17).

140

After God created human beings, he did not set them in a corner so that he could marvel at his creative masterpiece, as those who make porcelain dolls dress them beautifully and station them around their homes for guests to admire. God created us to be something like himself—that's why he gave us an assignment already in paradise.

When God created the cosmos, he viewed human beings as his coworkers who would fill the earth and use all of its marvelous realities. It's stunning what humanity can do. When we consider that a human being alone in a closed room can make calculations and produce equations and formulae that will actually place a human being on the moon, we realize that there is a mysterious connection between the way God put this world together and the way he put human beings together. God was pleased to make our minds something like his.

God is the Creator: his creative power was expressed in the fullest degree when he made the entire universe *out of nothing*. Human beings have creative powers too, in the field of art, in the field of design and architecture, in the field of ideas.

Just think about how we love to work. To be sure, people often dislike working for a living because they must work for other people and do unpleasant and arduous tasks. But look at the light in the eyes of those who have worked and produced something that is an expression of who they are. They will show you a cabinet they have made; they will show you a shawl they have crocheted; they will show you a story they have written; they will tell you of a scientific truth they have discovered; they will show you a watercolor they have painted. People without work fall into a state of mental confusion and physical degeneration; people who have work that excites them and fulfills them are buoyed up by God-given vigor each day.

God created us to work with him and for him. He recreated us in Christ so what he had in mind for us in the first place can be restored. He delights in his own work and the work of his children. Yes, when we get to heaven, we will sing a lot—but that's only part of the story.

In the meantime, believe in Christ as your Savior. And get ready, good friend, for glory, where you will be marvelously busy doing exactly what God will want you to do. You can be sure that what God wants you to do will be exactly what you want to do forever and ever.

Thank you, Lord Jesus, for dying so that we will be able truly to live forever. Lord Jesus, as we think about heaven, we are just trying to get it a little right. It is really going to be about working for you and your Father forever, isn't it? Amen.

SIXTY-EIGHT

Oddballs

Be transformed by the renewing of your mind.
—Romans 12:2

I vividly remember a conversation one evening with a pastor and his wife. We were talking about the impact of television on today's kids. We agreed that even shows that are relatively harmless come from the minds of people whose first desire is something other than furthering Christ's kingdom. And it's dangerous to let our children's minds be filled with what these creative types come up with. We all nodded and took another bite of cake and swallow of coffee. And then the pastor's wife said: "That's true . . . but I don't want my kids to be weird."

Exactly. No parents want their children to be weird, and nobody wants to be weird themselves. Everybody wants to be in the loop. Nobody wants to be an oddball. This is the reason we want our kids to watch the same television shows that other people watch, and this is the reason we make sure that we do the same. We don't want to be different—oddballs, dorks, nerds, whatever.

This can torpedo our spiritual lives.

Romans 12:1-2 is a passage we never stop thinking about while we are in this world. It comes after three chapters that teach us that salvation does "not depend on man's desire or effort but on God's mercy." God is the potter and we are the clay. All the chapters in Romans make us feel very small. God is the Savior. God is in charge of salvation 100 percent.

But then in chapter twelve, the tone suddenly changes. We are required to respond to God's saving grace by becoming oddballs. The Bible is a supremely realistic book— it recognizes that believers are living in a terrifically powerful world that has innumerable ways to make us conform to it. We must realize this, and we must resist.

The dear young mother who spoke of her desire for her children to conform to the general society expressed what is perhaps the most widely shared of all desires. No one wants to be different. Something inside all of us makes us want to be like everybody else. When people are talking together about the latest movie and the latest television sitcom, we want to be able to join in.

Many Christians become very skilled at covering over their uniquely Christian ideas and ways of looking at things. Conformity is the key to success in the world.

One of the characteristics of people who realize that they must already live in terms of their eternal future is that they are sensitive to the problem of conformity, and they devote their energy to dealing with it. Conformity to this world is spiritually debilitating. It can rob us of the full power and joy of our spiritual life. Conformity necessarily involves compromise, and compromise with wickedness is poison.

If we truly understand what had to happen in order for us to be saved by grace, then we have to take charge of our minds. The sovereign God who saves us summons us to oppose every force and power that tries to make us conform to the pattern of this world. Instead of conforming, we must work hard at mind renewal. That's the key. Every time the media try to make us think exactly as everyone else, we must resist. We must carefully monitor our lives to make sure that neither we nor our children are devoting blocks of time to influences that will make us conform to this world.

How do we resist these influences? By focusing our attention on God's will. How can we know God's will? By reading the Scriptures. When we read the Bible, we learn God's will and are equipped to keep it. We can choose to live with believers and seek to be like them, rather than like the world. And we can read literature that helps us understand the Bible and apply it to our daily lives.

People who have been transformed by such mind renewal will seem strange to others. They will not be able to participate in some conversations, because they will not know what the people are talking about. It's going to be very difficult for them to rear their children. There will be problems galore.

But the problems will be nothing compared to what's involved in being conformed to the pattern of this world.

Thank you, O Sovereign God, for saving us through your great mercy. Now help us respond as we should. Forgive us for wanting to conform to the pattern of this world. Through your Holy Spirit, help us work at the renewal of our minds. For Jesus' sake, Amen.

SIXTY-NINE

Think Pure

*Whatever is true, whatever is noble, whatever is right,
whatever is pure . . . think about such things.*
—Philippians 4:8

No one ever went broke underestimating the intelligence of the American people. We also know that no one ever goes broke when they cater to humanity's insatiable sexual appetite. Television, cinema, and the Internet are all cashing in. The United States Supreme Court recently announced that any attempt to curb some of the moral detritus offered at all times of the day—in the interest of protecting the innocence of children, let's say—is an improper limitation of free speech.

Moral corruption has never before been made available in so many ways. In fact, moral filth, deceit, and violence have become our environment. Many people do their best to protect their children, only to have them lose their innocence in five minutes on the Internet at the public library.

It's very possible that television and related media are the greatest single curse ever to befall the human race because they crawl into our skulls and take possession of our minds. They control what we think about. What people think about most of the time is not covered by any of the categories found in Philippians 4:8.

This means that those who think of themselves as eternal children of God and who think in eternal terms have an enormous problem. How can they possibly focus their minds on "whatever is true, whatever is noble, whatever is right, whatever is pure, whatever is lovely, whatever is admirable"—the praiseworthy things—when they are living in a sewer system?

The Bible issues this call to concentrate on worthwhile ideas near the end of a book that presents many of the profound teachings of Scripture, among them, one of the most moving descriptions of Jesus' humiliation. Paying attention to subjects that are admirable flows out of the great work of grace God has accomplished in Jesus Christ, his Son. Those who have faith in the Son and who want to follow him are simply going to have to distance themselves from what is happening around them.

What must we do to respond to this call? First of all, we should realize that we must have a solid foundation in the Christian faith itself. The apostle Paul calls us to these preoccupations immediately after writing this: "Whatever you have learned or received or heard from me, or seen in me—put it into practice." In other words the true, the noble, the right, the pure, the lovely follow from the message of Jesus' life, death, and resurrection.

What we need is total devotion to the Lord Jesus Christ and to the Bible. Having this, we will instinctively recognize that which is unworthy of our attention. When it appears on the screen, we will not find it entertaining but repulsive. The false, the ignoble, the wrong, the impure, and the indecent will make us turn away.

On the positive side, those who have a deep love for Christ must discipline themselves so that they will learn more about the Bible. There is so much we need to know in order to be Christians. There is so much we need to learn in order to follow Christ and understand the Bible; too much to allow for any time spent watching Oprah.

In addition, the Bible seems to be calling Christians to be interested in the development of art and music and architecture and good government—all the things that make our society a pleasant, even admirable place to live. About thirty-five hundred years ago, the Holy Spirit equipped Bezalel and Oholiab to do magnificent work on the tabernacle of God; with more than a ton of gold and nearly four tons of silver worked into its furnishings, it was beautiful. Christians then and now must use their skills to glorify God.

If we belong to Christ, if we think of this life as the beginning of an eternal experience with God himself, we will be different from those who are preoccupied with material that is unworthy of human beings. Our obedience to God requires us to be interested in what is good, what is true, and what is beautiful. And when we think only about those things, we can expect not to fit in very well.

O Lord, our minds are being attacked by the most vile enemies.
Look upon them and destroy what they are doing. Help us turn
away from all of the ugliness that prevails around us. Help us concentrate
on the true, the good, and the beautiful. For Jesus' sake, Amen.

SEVENTY

Experiencing Christ's Resurrection

Since, then, you have been raised with Christ,
set your hearts on things above, where Christ is. . . .
—Colossians 3:1

I f there is ever any doubt that those who believe in Christ are forever people, it should vanish whenever we read the opening verses of Colossians 3. Here we encounter a strange and revolutionary idea: ordinary men and women like us have experienced the resurrection along with Christ.

If this is actually true, obviously it is the greatest fact about anyone who believes in Christ. Christ rose from the dead, never to die again; within days he had ascended into heaven. If we have been raised with him, the benefits for us are indescribably magnificent.

When the Bible says that we have been raised with Christ, it does not mean that we simply share a common experience. We might say that we shared a fishing trip or a golf outing with Bill, but that would mean only that together we did the same thing at the same time. Being raised with Christ does not mean that he was raised and we were separately raised too, so that we have that experience in common. No, when the Bible tells us that we have been raised with Christ, it means that somehow we were "in" him. We were so identified with him when he rose from the dead that we actually experienced his resurrection.

The Bible frequently speaks of believers being "in" Christ. We are in Christ in two ways. First, he is our covenant head, our representative, so what he does affects us directly. Second, we are in Christ in terms of the mystical union—the real union we have with Christ through the work of the Holy Spirit in our lives.

We must learn to think of ourselves as being in Christ, and of him as being in us. In John 14:20, Christ Jesus, looking toward his coming in the Holy Spirit, told his followers: "On that day you will know that I am in my Father, and you are in me, and I am in you."

Let's take time out for a reality check. How often do we think about this? On Sundays it sometimes comes up. Maybe our devotional reading will sometimes remind us that we have been raised with Christ. But in all honesty, how often do we think about this? During the course of an ordinary day, ripping a board, closing a business deal, supervising a construction crew, making blueprints, wiping our kids' noses, mopping the floor—how often do we think about this?

We have to develop some mind control here. To start with, we need to develop a prayer life that lives out of the reality of our union with Christ and our resurrection with him. We need to continuously ask God to make us aware of this great truth.

All sorts of practical matters flow out of the fact that we have been raised together with Christ. The first is simply that we ourselves are involved in a post-resurrection life right now. That means that what we are doing right now has something to do with eternity. It means that we can start laying up treasures in heaven. We can start doing things that give God pleasure and make the devil angry as hell.

There's a song that children and adults love to sing: "Seek ye first the kingdom of God and his righteousness, and all these things will be added unto you. Allelu, Alleluia." Makes good sense. But we really need Colossians 3:1 to actually accomplish this kind of kingdom seeking. The same sentence that reminds us that we have been raised with Christ then tells us to set our hearts on the "things that are above, where Christ is seated at the right hand of God."

If we would just remember what has happened to us—*if we would just remember*—then obviously we would be thinking of Christ and his will for us every moment. Resurrection is an event that makes people eternal and transports them into heaven. Since we were raised with Christ, we should be thinking of him and trying our level best to do his will. We should be praying all the time that we will recognize his will and do it, almost naturally, with the help of his Holy Spirit.

Yes, we are forever people. This is no figure of speech; it is reality. Once we have been raised with Christ, everything is oriented differently. We keep looking at the throne room, at the throne; in fact, we're on the throne from which the universe is governed. And the King is with us and in us right now.

Our poor minds, O Christ, are still not grasping what you are telling us today. Just help us say, "I believe this is true." And gradually, over time, make us into people who want nothing more than to do your heavenly will each day. Amen.

SEVENTY-ONE

First Things

*"But seek first his kingdom and his righteousness,
and all these things will be given to you as well."*
—Matthew 6:33

I f we seek our heavenly Father's kingdom and his righteousness, we will have
enough to eat, enough to drink, enough to wear, and adequate housing. Now,
that's a pretty good deal, isn't it? So why don't we do just that?

We don't seek our Father's kingdom first because doing so won't provide us with
a new boat, a six-thousand-square-foot house, fine cuisine, fabulous vacations, and a
Land Rover with on-board navigation tied into a satellite.

When Jesus told his followers that seeking his Father's kingdom would provide
them with an adequate benefit package, he was talking to people for whom food
and drink, shelter and clothing were a problem. Ninety-five percent of the people
figured that if they had these, they were home free. Only a few people were wealthy.

Today it's different. When Jesus talks to us about the benefit package that goes
along with seeking the Father's kingdom first, we say to ourselves: He just doesn't
understand. We are living in a time when we can have all sorts of toys: Harleys,
RVs, swimming pools, great cars, a house and a trailer at the lake. In all honesty, the
food and drink and clothing thing isn't a big deal anymore; we can take care of that
by ourselves very easily.

Oh, we are in big trouble. Reading the Bible in the materialistic environment we
live in all the time is a huge problem. Because biblical language calls us to totally
revise our thinking and remake our attitudes, we usually let the really tough stuff
float over our heads. Or we let our kids sing about it at church school: "Seek ye first

the kingdom of God, and his righteousness"—you know how the song goes. And they sing it very well.

When I talk with those who have regular contact with the church in so-called developing countries, they often tell me that they are shamed by the quality of faith they find. Here are people who are thankful with enough to eat and drink, enough clothing and adequate shelter, and they are entirely willing to do business with their heavenly Father on Jesus' terms. They have no safety net beneath them; if they become seriously ill, they will likely die. But they think about their Savior much more than we do, they pray with a fervency we cannot begin to duplicate, and they seek first things first.

Yes, indeed, we do have a big problem, and the really troubling thing about our problem is this: we don't think it is a problem. When we prosper and we are showered with more things than we know what to do with, we are apt to say very piously, "Oh, the Lord has blessed us so wonderfully." Well, that's a good thing to say, and it's even true. But we must also face the fact that, unless we are alert to the dire danger here, we are apt to become people who really don't think about seeking our Father's kingdom first. To be sure, we do seek it second; after we have created our own little kingdom of bright shiny things that go fast or look good, we make sure that we give something to our Father's kingdom.

We who know the Bible well and who can recite what Jesus said about seeking the kingdom in a heartbeat—it just rolls off our tongues—must realize that we are in grave spiritual danger. It is simply a fact that material things can become our idols, and we devote our lives to maintaining them, improving them, and getting more of them. Prosperous parents infect their children with the virus of materialism, and so it goes, on and on and on.

My computer has an auto-correct feature that automatically corrects mistakes I make in spelling, even in grammar. Well, materialistic believers have something like that working for them when they read the Bible. As they read the words, their own "auto-correct" takes the text and changes it a little or leaves some of it out—whatever is necessary so that it will not actually change their lives. They do whatever is necessary so that they will be able to keep on seeking another kingdom first, before they give their attention to their heavenly Father's.

I must listen to Jesus, really listen. And I must figure out what his words mean for me when he tells me to concentrate on first things first. It's not easy.

Heavenly Father, it is true: your kingdom is the most important reality in the universe. Please forgive our materialism. Father, it will take your miracle to change us. We want to be changed, and yet we don't. Please help us. Amen.

SEVENTY-TWO

Schizoid Christians

When I want to do good, evil is right there with me.
—Romans 7:21

When William headed for Sioux Falls, he drove like a madman. He didn't take his meds that morning; he resented his meds. Every time he took them it was like all of his enemies getting into his head. He called them his enemies; they were actually people who loved him dearly, and he knew they did, but they were always telling him what to do. And then the voices told him to go and go fast, very fast—on the Interstate. Go! Go! Go! When he crashed in Nebraska, one of his enemies came to get him and bring him home. His Camaro was totaled.

William is a schizophrenic. I understand him very well. I am a schizophrenic too. So was the apostle Paul.

Maybe it's unfair to talk about my problem and Paul's as if they are the same as William's, who is, by the way, a composite I've created from some of the schizophrenics I know. But there are similarities. Eternal people, forever people who know that Christ is in them through his Spirit and who know that everything they do in this world has eternal consequences, hear bad voices too.

Perhaps they are not as loud as the voices schizophrenics hear—they don't have to be. They come into our consciousness on the deepest level, virtually inaudible but strong nonetheless. Sometimes the voices taunt us, asking why we believe as we do. Sometimes they ask us to consider doing things that other people would never imagine us considering. Sometimes they tell us things about others that we shouldn't think.

In Romans 7, none other than the apostle Paul tells of his own experience with what he calls elsewhere "the old self," which is characterized by deceitful desires

(Eph. 4:23). This old self is the opposite of the new nature that the Holy Spirit has created inside him. But this opposite self is not completely destroyed while we are in this world. In fact, one of the great prospects of the "forever" that we will experience beyond the grave is that we will finally be rid of this old nature completely. But meanwhile, while we are here . . .

Yes, while we are here, this old self keeps talking to us, sometimes while we are sitting in church, sometimes when we have settled down for prayer all by ourselves with the door closed. It is the meanest, most inconsiderate pest. Sometimes it embarrasses us. Often it makes us go to God and clench our fists and grind our teeth and call out, "Please, oh please be merciful to me—there's still so much sin in me, and I cannot seem to get rid of it totally."

Some people think that when Christians are tempted like this, it's a devil in them that is doing it. But there is good reason to believe that devils don't get inside Christian believers and talk to them. Devils know that Christians are off-limits for them; they belong to Christ, and they have the sign of Jesus' blood that identifies them as belonging to him. So when the temptations come from inside, we cannot blame Satan for that; we have only ourselves to blame.

In Romans 7, the apostle Paul does not blame the devil for the voice he hears that tells him to do exactly what he knows he should not do. No, it's the law of sin that still resides within him, that part of his nature that is not yet sanctified. And so the war goes on and on and on.

Thank God, God has given us everything we need to resist this old nature. The old nature is there, and when it speaks to us, it reminds us that it has not yet retired and died; but we don't have to listen to it. Schizophrenics who learn to live with the voices they hear learn to distinguish between the ugly voices from inside and the voices they should listen to. So too, those who want to follow Christ and do his will because they know they are building for eternity learn to tell the difference between the suggestions that come from their old self and the leading of the Holy Spirit.

The apostle concludes Romans 7 with a shout of anguish: "What a wretched man I am! Who will rescue me from this body of death?" (v. 24). Ah . . . the answer is so clear. Jesus will. So Paul writes of the victory believers may have in the chapter that follows: "You . . . are controlled not by the sinful nature but by the Spirit, if the Spirit of God lives in you" (Rom. 8:9).

Lord Jesus, you know us perfectly, and you know that things are going on inside our heads that bother us terribly. We are still sinful people, there's no doubt about that. Forgive us, we pray, and control us in this day by the Spirit of holiness. Amen.

SEVENTY-THREE

Wretched Travelers

What a wretched man I am! Who will rescue me from this body of death?
—Romans 7:24

Have you ever been jealous of the thief who became a Christ-believer on the cross and saw Christ in glory that very day? You can measure how long he was a Christian on earth in minutes.

Sometime I envy him, not because I want to live like the devil until just before the bell, but because he never had to feel the wretchedness Paul talks about in Romans 7. Believers who live on earth for a while will have days when we want to scream, WHY CAN'T I BE A BETTER CHRISTIAN?

It would be so nice if the line on the graph of our Christian lives would move steadily upward until we finally see Christ. But that's not the way it is. The line is more like the chart that marks the Dow Jones—it jiggles all over the place, occasionally reaching new highs and also, more than occasionally, reaching new lows.

One of the treasures believers have is the apostle Paul's candid journal of his own feelings. Why did the Holy Spirit preserve so much information about this man? Don't you think it was because he understood the gospel better than anyone before or since, and his reaction to it was classic? We should expect that some of the same feelings Paul expresses are going to distress us. Romans 7 reveals his inner conflict so dramatically that some have erroneously concluded that he was describing what he was before he became a Christian.

Serious followers of Christ have to deal with God's law while they are in this world. For our purposes just now, we may think of that law as the Ten Commandments. In addition, we have the love law, which captures their essence—love God with all you are and love your neighbor as if you were standing in his shoes.

Romans 7 describes the apostle's intense disappointment with himself because of his failure to keep the law of God, in spite of his best intentions. He is ashamed and embarrassed because he realizes that there is something inside him that takes God's good law and uses it exactly as it should not be used.

On the one hand, the law provides a useful service: it identifies sin for us. Paul uses the example of coveting to illustrate this. He says, "I would not have known what coveting really was if the law had not said, "Do not covet." Yes, that's how dumb we have become—we cannot even identify sin unless the law puts a label on an action or a way of thinking and says, "That's stealing, stupid." Or "That's adultery, stupid." When we live in an environment that reeks of sin and something inside us resonates to all of it, it's easy to sin without realizing it.

On the other hand, when we learn that a certain deed is evil, it seems as if this knowledge sets an engine in motion inside us that makes us want to do exactly what we are told not to do. It's like what happens when a mother goes next door and, just before she goes, she tells her children, "While I'm talking to Mrs. Miller, don't you dare eat any of those chocolate chippers I just baked."

We're like children. Don't steal—but now that you mention it, Lord, it would certainly help things if I did; let's see now—if I took a few more deductions, the IRS would likely never notice.

Don't commit adultery—but now that you mention it, Lord, I wouldn't mind spending a little bit more time with Ashley at the office—at least she doesn't get on my case about cleaning the crawl space like the Ashley I married does.

We are, sad to say, a cursed race, and there's sin inside us. It was if there were two Pauls. One was "old-nature" Paul; that was the Paul of the sinful flesh. "We know that the law is spiritual; but I am unspiritual" (v. 14). He keeps calling this unspiritual element in his life "flesh." His "inner being"—his mind—loves God's law and wants to do it. But, he says, "I see another law at work in the members of my body, waging war against the law of my mind and making me a prisoner of the law of sin at work within my members" (v. 23).

And that's what makes him shriek in anguish, "What a wretched man I am!" Then he looks into Christ's face and realizes once again that Christ and Christ alone can deliver him from the wretched battle that is making his life so miserable.

O Jesus, how we need you! We need you before we come to that point of surrender to you, and we need you after you have captured us and made us your own. The battle just keeps going on inside us. Forgive us our sin, and help us in our struggle. Thank you, O Jesus Christ, our Lord. Amen.

SEVENTY-FOUR

"Stinkin' Thinkin'"

No one who is born of God will continue to sin, because God's seed remains in him; he cannot go on sinning. . . .
—1 John 3:9

Human abilities are mind-boggling. Advances in science fill us with awe. Works of art and literature are often marvelous. The human mind is exquisite and glorious. And it excels especially in dreaming up ways to justify sin.

The book of 1 John was written to believers who were dealing with a really clever way to justify sin. A teaching called Gnosticism was floating around and touching the early church. The name isn't important. What's important was that the capital "G" provided believers with a way they could think of themselves as believers even though they would sometimes visit a brothel.

Here's how that works: Gnosticism connects everything that has to do with your religion with your soul, the nonmaterial part of your person. That leaves your body free to do what it pleases. What you do with your body doesn't really make any difference. The possibilities are endless. Enjoy!

Finding ways to excuse sin is the best-developed of all human skills. And just because a person becomes a believer in Christ does not mean that that skill is forgotten. The apostle Paul dealt with Christians who came up with another smart way to justify sin: Let's sin so that grace will increase. Clever. Very clever.

The words of 1 John 3 that declare that those who are born of God cannot sin must be seen as God's reaction to our ability to excuse our sin. Through the apostle John, God tells us that whenever we consider the possibility of sinning, we must immediately stop thinking about it. We must put it out of our mind. There is no justification for it. None. None whatsoever.

First John 3:8-10 lays it out very clearly: What is born of God cannot sin. There is no place in the Christian life for sin and sinning. It must be rooted out. It may not even be considered. We may not find clever ways to justify our sin. Sin is of the devil, it is not of God. Jesus has come to destroy the devil's works. "No one who is born of God will continue to sin, because God's seed remains in him; he cannot go on sinning, because he has been born of God."

Christians experience temptations to sin in two ways. The most obvious way is from the outside; we live in an environment that is dominated by realities and influences that tempt us away from God. The entertainment industry—to name just one example—exerts great influence on all of us, especially because it is available in our homes through videos, television, and the Internet. Believers are tempted from the outside nowadays as never before.

But we are also tempted from the inside because of the residue of the old self that remains in us. No one is entirely sanctified while in this world. In fact, as the book of 1 John tells us, "If we claim to be without sin, we deceive ourselves and the truth is not in us" (1:8). It is this sin within us that continues to play nasty games with us. The temptation to sin that comes from within, possibly leftovers from an earlier non-Christian lifestyle, are often accompanied by the thinking we use to justify falling back into them again even though we are Christians. Alcoholics call this "stinkin' thinkin,'" and that's a good name for it.

Stinkin' thinkin' is any thinking that believers use to justify playing games with sin in any way, shape, or form. When temptation to sin comes, either from the outside or the inside, we must remember that we have been born of God. God is righteous and holy. What has been born of God cannot sin. It is an impossible idea. When temptation comes, the very next thought a true believer must have is that it is out of the question. It is unthinkable because sin is of the devil, and if we have been born of God, we are of God.

It would be nice if those who became Christians would never sin again. Sorry, but that doesn't happen. Sin is too pervasive in the culture around us and within our own hearts. But those who have truly been born again can stop making excuses and must stop formulating elaborate justification for going on with their sinful ways. There is no justification for sin whatsoever. There was none when Adam stammered outside Eden, and there is none today. When it comes to sin, there is just one thing to do: fight. Just fight and resist in the power of Almighty God.

Holy God, help us stop doing what we are so very good at: justifying sin even though we believe in you. We confess that often we toy with the idea of sinning. It's so alluring. Please forgive us and change us. We pray in Christ's name, Amen.

SEVENTY-FIVE

The Alibi Agency

*He was assigned a grave with the wicked . . . though he had done no violence,
nor was any deceit in his mouth.*
—Isaiah 53:9

Of all the exhibits that illustrate the degradation of our time, few are more degenerate than a company called Alibi Agency. The *Atlantic Monthly* article that described it presented it as a clever organization. That's true, but its very cleverness portrays how dominant falsehood is nowadays.

Alibi Agency, based in Blackpool, England, establishes a paper trail and whatever other data is necessary for unfaithful spouses to prove to their suspicious husbands or wives that they have indeed been engaged in honest activities, when in fact they have been desecrating their marriage. *Atlantic* reports that the agency "will furnish ticket stubs for the theater performance you were supposed to have been attending. It will print up dummy invitations to the social and business events that kept you away from home. It will hire official-sounding receptionists who will intercept phone calls to the putative locale of your out-of-town conference or golf game."

The aim of the agency is "total peace of mind" for the erring spouses it serves. It invites prospective clients to discus their needs so that the agency will be able to tailor the alibis to their specifications.

It is likely true that only the very rich could possibly afford the services of this organization. What is so sad, though, is that many people really don't need its services. Think of how often we make our own alibis—we change things, shade the truth, fudge on our performance in order to give certain people the impression we want them to receive, not necessarily the truth. And think of the way deceit operates in business. Without actually lying, there are clever ways to convey impressions and facts that are actually inaccurate and untrue.

When we go back about 2,600 years before Alibi Agency was formed, we find a description of Jesus Christ that emphasizes his absolute truthfulness. Isaiah 53 is a remarkable prophecy about the coming Messiah that stuns us with its detail. Of the coming Messiah, it declares that there was no deceit in his mouth.

It is possible to establish a wide range of contrasts between our sinful selves and the person of Jesus Christ, but this is one of the most basic: he is not deceitful, but we are. It is difficult for us to tell the truth. Most of us become skilled deceivers because we begin by deceiving ourselves. Who among us are able to face the realities about our person without flinching? We use uncounted psychological mechanisms and tricks to convey false impressions about ourselves to ourselves. We mask our laziness, our greed, our lust, our rebellion against God and succeed in convincing ourselves that we come about as close as anyone could to Adam or Eve in the state of integrity.

How old are children before they begin to lie? Two years old? Earlier? Maybe earlier. We are born with a mechanism inside us that senses when it is better to lie than tell the truth. In normal children, this mechanism is seldom the last to develop. And as we progress through grade school and high school we discover that it is often better to waffle on the truth than tell it straight.

This does not mean that most of us are pathological liars, nor even that most of us are eager to learn the website of Alibi Agency. Not at all. What I am referring to is the quick way we sense when the real truth will be detrimental to us, and we withhold one or more facts and spin the data somewhat. We do whatever is necessary so that we will not be hurt as we would be if the real truth were known.

So it is that the prophet Isaiah, writing at the Holy Spirit's prompting, described the fundamental difference between Christ Jesus and us very simply: there was no deceit in his mouth, while our mouths are full of it. Not even flossing helps.

Jesus is the only truthful person who ever walked this earth. There was none other who told the truth as he did. He told it because he knew the truth fully. So today again, we must turn to him and ask him to enlighten us with the truth we need to know, about ourselves, about the God who is the Father of Christ, and about the way this holy God saves deceitful people like us.

As we turn to Christ, we are cleansed from our lifelong love affair with deceit. And he gives us his blessed Spirit so that we can begin to tell the truth, first to ourselves, then to others. We need a truthful Savior, and we have one.

O holy God, we confess that our mouths are often full of deceit.
We are so grateful that your Son has come to show us the way of truth.
Please forgive us our deceit, and create us anew so that we
become honest as Christ is honest. In his name, Amen.

SEVENTY-SIX

What Joseph Saw

"How then could I do such a wicked thing and sin against God?"
—Genesis 39:9

One of the most remarkable events in the Bible is Joseph's refusal to go to bed with Potiphar's wife. We must assume that she was an attractive woman; a high Egyptian official would have none other. She was insistent. But he refused. Steadfastly. He refused, he said, because he simply couldn't sin against God in this way.

What is so astonishing about this situation is that it should have turned out entirely differently. Joseph was a young man, he had grown up in a topsy-turvy family that had rejected him most cruelly. He had plunged from the position of favored son to lowly slave. But what is most interesting is that this event occurred more than four hundred years before the Ten Commandments were given to the Israelites; they were not posted in Joseph's school. He had never heard the commandment "You shall not commit adultery."

Of course, there are clear indications that even before the Ten Commandments were given, the human conscience was tuned in such a way that most people realized that it was wrong to take another man's wife. Even so, conscience alone does not explain why Joseph steered clear of his boss's wife.

When we read the story of Joseph's life, we discover that this man had an exceptionally clear understanding of the importance of human relationships. When Potiphar's wife kept after him, he arranged his schedule so that he would not even see her. And when she continued her seduction and cornered him, he reminded her that her husband, his master, had given him a position of exceptional trust: "Everything he owns he has entrusted to my care." The only thing he had not given to him was his wife. So he could not do what she suggested—he simply couldn't do it—because of the social relationships that were in place. They could not be violated; they could not be broken.

We should notice this carefully. Sexual immorality is not wrong because there is something intrinsically wrong with sexual activity itself; instead, sexual immorality is so reprehensible because it destroys the fabric of society. If Joseph had entered into an illicit relationship with Potiphar's wife, it would have created an abominable situation. Even if they had never been discovered, their contact with each other would have been seriously corrupted.

Joseph's steadfast refusal was based on his understanding that bad sex causes a bad life in many ways and on many levels. God is primarily interested in social relationships among his people. These relationships must be kept pure and unblemished. In fact, all of the commandments in the last table of the law (commandments five through ten) are there to protect the social relationships that are essential if a society is going to hold together.

All of the Ten Commandments can be summarized in terms of the concept of love. The first table of the law teaches us how to have a proper relationship with God: we must love God with all that we are. The second table teaches us how to establish proper relationships with our family, and it also protects our relationships within the rest of society. We are not to cut people up with our gossip; we are to honor the property rights of others; and we are not to kill people, not even before they are born. All of this is designed to create human relationships that are strong, wholesome, and good.

Nowadays people are so shortsighted that they think of sin in terms of the short-term pleasures it offers them and the possible risks they take when they indulge themselves. They fail to see that in the Bible's view, sin destroys the fabric of human society. Relationships between husbands and wives, parents and children, children and children, children and parents, neighbors with neighbors, employers and employees—all of these must be protected. Lying, stealing, abusing children, and sleeping around corrupt all these and make life awkward and embarrassing . . . and evil in the sight of God.

Joseph never heard of the seventh commandment, but he realized that if he were to succumb to Mrs. Potiphar's seductions, he would have ruined social relationships, which he viewed as sacred. These relationships are still sacred, and we may not, we must not, destroy them.

Creator God, you have put society together so that it is very delicate and vulnerable. Help us avoid sexual immorality and other sinfulness because of what it does to our relationship with you and with others. For Jesus' sake, Amen.

SEVENTY-SEVEN

Eternal Fathers

*I have chosen him, so that he will direct his children
and his household after him to keep the way of the LORD.*
—Genesis 18:19

P eter Reese Doyle figures that if you can get dads to do their duty, everything
will work out just fine. He's an author of a series of children's books about the
Revolutionary War, books that promote a biblical philosophy of life. He's also
pastor of a Presbyterian church in Opilika, Alabama. Doyle told me that he spends
a lot of time with the men of his church. I think he's right about fathers.

Creating a Christian home and environment in which children mature and grow
is not just women's work, though their role is enormous. In the Bible, everything
starts with the father. And if we ever doubted that, we should take a close look at
the scene described in Genesis 18.

There we find the Lord and Abraham walking toward the cities of the plain,
Sodom and Gomorrah. The Lord is turning things over in his mind, wondering
whether he should be totally up-front with Abraham and tell him exactly what he is
going to do. He concludes that he should and he will. The reason is very interesting: "I have chosen him, so that he will direct his children and his household after
him to keep the way of the Lord by doing what is right and just, so that the LORD
will bring about for Abraham what he has promised him."

The Lord was thinking about his friend Abraham in contrast to the moral degradation of the cities of the plain. Within hours, the angels who accompanied the
Lord and Abraham would enter Sodom, where the citizens would attempt to assault
them; there they would rescue Abraham's nephew Lot and his stubborn wife and
corrupt daughters. In Sodom, fathers and sons and daughters were caught in the
embrace of a foul sexuality that dominated everything. As God thinks about

Abraham, he reminds himself that he chose Abraham to be the father of a special people who would be different from the inhabitants of those doomed cities.

Isn't it mind-boggling that the Bible actually sometimes tells us what goes on in God's mind? In this case, when God was thinking about Abraham, he was also thinking about what is involved in fatherhood.

If any group of people need the ability to multi-task, it surely must be fathers. Fathers have a wide range of responsibilities, especially these days: they have to support their families financially, do a good job at work, and, if they are active members of the church, accomplish tasks in the church as well. But these many responsibilities must never obscure their primary responsibility: directing their children and their household.

We must not allow the exceptional nature of the events described here to obscure the extremely important statement about fatherhood found in Genesis 18. We are apt to slide over it. But we must not. We learn here what believing fathers must have uppermost on their minds at all times. As they live their eternal lives already in this world, they must direct their children and their household.

This does not mean that they simply point everybody in the right direction, give them a gentle shove, and then assume that everything will be okay. The word used here refers to giving children (and their wives too) explicit directives. It's the same word used when God commanded Adam and Eve not to eat of the forbidden tree in Eden. The *direction* referred to here is about communication—it's about telling children exactly what is expected of them. Fathers are to give direction as representatives of the Lord himself. God wanted Abraham to tell his children the way of the Lord. The object of this direction is not just to have good kids who do all right in school and don't embarrass their parents in the neighborhood. Rather, it is to have children who do what is right and just in the sight of God.

The only fathers who can do this are those who are themselves living close to Christ. Very close. They must be men of prayer, faithful in Bible reading and study. They must attend worship services where the Word of God is central and set an example with their lives of what they want their children to be.

When believing fathers direct their children and their households in this way, they and their children will see the promises of God fulfilled in their lives.

Pastor Doyle is correct: if dads do their God-given duty, everything will turn out fine.

O Lord who walked with Abraham, help us to get our priorities straight in our families. Help us pass on your directives to our dear children so that they, your church, and our nation may benefit, and you will be glorified. Amen.

SEVENTY-EIGHT

Husband Love

*Husbands, love your wives, just as Christ
loved the church and gave himself up for her.*
—Ephesians 5:25

When it comes to marriage, the Bible is a disappointment. That is, it doesn't provide us with many good examples of marriage. Actually, it gives details of quite a few marriages that were less than ideal.

Abraham's marriage wasn't ideal. He did some things to his wife, Sarah, that were very inconsiderate. Like the times he told her to say she was his sister when they were in Egypt and later when they stayed in Gerar, where King Abimelech ruled. Sure enough, the king of Egypt took her into his harem, and so did Abimelech. I don't want to detract from Abraham in any way, but if you are looking for an ideal marriage, you will have to look elsewhere.

Not until we get to the New Testament, after the Holy Spirit was poured out, do we begin to see the full beauty of marriage as God intended it to be. In order to have a good marriage, both partners really need to believe the Bible, love Christ and have his Spirit in their hearts, and want to live in their marriage the way God tells them to live.

The key to a really great marriage is the love a husband has for his wife. Don't misunderstand me here. The wife's love in the marriage is necessary too, but it is husband love described in the Bible that makes Christian marriage unique. I use the word *unique* deliberately. Unbelievers marry too, and sometimes their marriages are good. But unbelievers can never have marriages like those of believing husbands and believing wives. When husband and wife are both believers, their marriage reflects a divine reality. That reality is the relationship of Jesus Christ and his church.

What we find in Ephesians 5 about marriage contradicts most modern views of marriage. In fact, it contradicts most modern views of gender and the relationships of men and women. Nowadays the operative idea is *egalitarianism*. In this view, men and women are interchangeable. Two women can adopt a child; so can two men. In marriage, the husband and wife are on an equal footing, both are equally in charge of the marriage and the family. The biblical view is different. It says that husbands have special responsibilities for their wives' well-being. Husbands are to love their wives as Christ loved the church.

People who view their lives in the light of eternity think of marriage differently from the modern ideas of marriage. They remember that the greatest thing going on in our world right now is that the bride is getting ready for the bridegroom. They know that history can be described as what goes on in the dressing room when the bride is getting ready to march down the aisle to be married to her husband.

The Bible calls the church the bride of Christ, and it calls Christ the bridegroom. The language in Ephesians 5 reflects this idea. There we learn that Christ gave himself up for the church "to make her holy, cleansing her by the washing with water through the word, and to present her to himself as a radiant church, without stain or wrinkle or any other blemish, but holy and blameless" (vv. 26-27).

All our marriage problems would disappear if women would make sure that the men they marry love Christ and want to love them as Christ loved the church. They would all disappear if men would make Christ's sacrificial love for his church their great example.

Jesus suffered, bled, and died for his church, and he suffered and bled and died for the marriages of his people. No man can love his wife as Christ loved the church unless the Holy Spirit comes into his heart and enables him to do so.

What we need to know about great marriages is found in the New Testament, after the Holy Spirit was given to God's people. Now that the Holy Spirit has been poured out on us, husbands can love their wives as Christ loves the church—not perfectly, but they can make a good beginning. When husbands do that, marriages last and last and last.

Lord Jesus, we men are not accustomed to thinking of ourselves as your bride, but we are part of your bride when we believe in you. Thank you for loving us so much that you died for us, and now you care for us perfectly. Help husbands to love their wives the way you love your bride. Amen.

SEVENTY-NINE

Hosea Love

"Go, show your love to your wife again,
though she is loved by another and is an adulteress."
—Hosea 3:1

Those whose minds and ideas are formed by the Bible rather than by modern opinions will act in a unique way as married people. Unfortunately, there is no escaping the power of the modern lifestyle that creeps uninvited into our homes. No marriage is safe. When pastors prepare couples for marriages, they cannot help but look into their eyes and wonder, Will they stay together?

They find themselves asking this question even of those for whom it seems as if every condition for a good marriage has been met: the couple are old enough to be married, they have known each other for a long time and have been serious about being married for a year or two, and they share a common faith in Christ.

We live in an age in which adultery is in the air we breathe; it is a time that duplicates the age just before the flood judgment rolled over the earth and destroyed every air-breathing beast. "The LORD saw how great man's wickedness on the earth had become, and that every inclination of the thoughts of his heart was only evil all the time" (Gen. 6:5).

It is wacky how a spouse who has always been faithful can change. Sometimes it happens overnight: a woman who has been a good wife and mother will start hanging around bars, looking for excitement with anyone who comes along. A husband may do the same. And so marriages bust up. Smithereens. People grieving with a grief worse than death, betrayed teenage children who vow never to get married themselves—these are part of the ghastly residue.

What's the answer? Why, divorce, of course, some say.

Not necessarily. When we live by the Scriptures, we discover that adultery is not enough to demand that a husband and wife dissolve their marriage and go their separate ways. God tells the prophet Hosea, "Go, take to yourself an adulterous wife" (1:2). So he marries Gomer. Sometimes God communicates his message to us through a preacher or through one person telling the gospel to another, sometimes through a drama. God chooses the actors and directs them through each scene. In this case, God tells Hosea to marry Gomer in order to show what God himself had done when he "married" his bride, the nation of Israel. Gomer was not a virtuous woman, nor was Israel a virtuous bride for Almighty God.

The book of Hosea reports Gomer's repeated infidelities and tells of God's repeated wooing of adulterous Israel: "Therefore I am now going to allure her; I will lead her into the desert and speak tenderly to her. There I will give her back her vineyards, and will make the Valley of Achor a door of hope. There she will sing as in the days of her youth, as in the day she came up out of Egypt" (3:14-15).

Then God says to the prophet, "Go back to Gomer, and love her as the Lord loves the people of Israel." In New Testament language this would read, "Go back to your unfaithful wife, and love her just as Christ loves the church." Christian husbands and wives have to think deeply about this, and so does the Christian community, which is so often torn by marriage collapse. Sometimes adultery appears where we least expect it. But divorce must not be the first reaction. Even when a legal divorce is in place because of the insistence of the adulterous partner, the other partner should not necessarily consider the marriage over. The laws of God are more important than the laws of humankind.

I felt the power of this idea when I had lunch with a man whose divorce had been in place for nearly a year. "I see you still wear your wedding ring," I said. "Yes," he replied. "I believe that in the sight of God we are still married." A few days later, he went to woo his errant wife once more.

For believers, marriage must always be viewed as a dramatic representation of God's relationship with his beloved people. The world considers us nuts for thinking like this. Let them so think. The Bible is clear: God loved Israel in spite of her repeated adulteries. His words to Hosea—"Go, show your love to your wife again . . . though she is an adulteress"—reflect God's own love for his people.

All he asks when he says to never give up on a marriage is that we imitate him. When we do that, we may be sure that God will help us. He will answer our prayers.

O Loving God, we who are your bride confess with deep contrition that we are an adulterous people. Thank you for loving still, for wooing us with the blessed gospel. Thank you for being our loving husband. O Lord, have mercy. For Jesus' sake, Amen.

EIGHTY

The Forgiving Mode

Forgive as the Lord forgave you.
—Colossians 3:13

Those who pray the Lord's prayer each day and model all their prayers after it ultimately become people who are very different from those who don't pray.

If Jesus were to talk with us about his prayer, he would likely ask, "Does this prayer surprise you?" And if we'd reply, "Yes . . . in a way, it does," he might say rather sharply, "It's meant to surprise you, especially the item about forgiveness. Did you notice the way I connected my Father's forgiving you with your forgiving others?"

God's forgiveness of sinners is a major biblical theme, stretching from the debacle in paradise to the Bible's last chapter. That forgiveness depends solely on God's love and willingness to endure measureless suffering. And the perfect prayer, to our surprise, ties this grand theme into our personal lives.

No day, no hour should go by without our remembering that God wants us to forgive as he has forgiven us. If believers would remember this principle and live it, the pathetic personal relationship problems that plague their marriages, their families, and the churches they attend would vanish.

Jesus himself was so taken by the connection between divine and human forgiveness that he returned to this theme as soon as he finished the prayer itself. And his story of the unmerciful servant (Matt. 18:21-35) reinforces the requirement that forgiven people must become forgiving people. The despicable servant gladly accepted the cancellation of his large debt, only to turn and demand payment from all who owed him. So his debt was reinstated and he was thrown into prison "to be tortured." Jesus then made this withering announcement: "This is how your heavenly Father will treat each of you unless you forgive your brother from your heart."

Possibly we've got it all wrong. We think of forgiveness as an act when we should think of it as a mode of life. We think of forgiving others in terms of specific damage others have done to our egos, our positions, and our possessions.

Surely we are required to forgive specific really crummy things people have done to us. But we can best honor the principle that we should forgive just as God in Christ has forgiven us if we adopt a mode that makes forgiveness our characteristic response to every wrong, however petty, that comes our way. Life does not consist of long stretches of vanilla pudding days in which nothing ever happens to make us angry, punctuated by rare occasions when someone says something or does something that makes us mad as hops. Usually, we live with people who have little ways of getting under our skin—they do inconsiderate things, their habits drive us up the wall. These pesky interruptions of our good humor can sometimes become unbearable on the days we feel desolate ourselves.

It would be nice if this unpleasantness were confined to the workplace, but unfortunately our families and our marriages also suffer their share of the daily, hourly, wrongs we perpetrate on one another. Don't think God is unaware of this. The Father had to send his Son to forgive people like us who are experts at making life miserable for our traveling companions. Now God wants us to shift to the forgiving mode and not shift out of it.

That means that because I am a forgiven sinner, no one—not my children, my wife, the people I work with, the people in my congregation—is going to be able to do anything that alienates us from each other. No one. I am a forgiven sinner, after all, so you cannot make me vengeful, no matter what you do to me, no matter what you say of me. Believe that?

It would be nice if that were true. So why isn't it? Because of our lack of faith, because we do not spend enough time thinking about what God has done for us in Christ. We take our own forgiveness for granted. We figure that God had to forgive us, since we have been kind enough to believe in him. We consider our selves spiritually superior to others. But woe to those who insult us, who question our motives, who don't do what we expect them to do—we shall not forget.

Being in the forgiving mode will rescue us from this wretched condition and will save us from being "tortured" as the unmerciful servant was.

O Christ, let me never forget what you had to do in order that my debt could be paid. Help me to forgive the big things people have done to me, but above all, help me live in the forgiving mode. Amen.

EIGHTY-ONE

The Note of Joy

I have told you this so that my joy may be in you
and that your joy may be complete.
—John 15:11

When I talked with Bill about his son who had strayed a long way from Christ, we both wondered aloud why. The boy knew what there was to know—Christian grade school and high school, Sunday school and countless sermons. But here he was, crowding thirty, a failed marriage, several years of blind drunkenness and now, thankfully, his life coming back together—but no interest in the church. None. Zilch. Why?

"Well," Bill said, sort of as an afterthought, "when he talks about the church, he always mentions all the fighting going on." Hmmm. . . . Maybe that's it.

Maybe? No maybe about it.

The church being what it is—the pillar and ground of truth—has to be a place where error is resisted and God's truth is proclaimed. And the church being what it is—a communion of saints who are not entirely sanctified—is bound to experience differences of opinion among the members and a little strife once in a while.

If the impression we give our youngsters as they grow up is that we are always fighting, somebody better call a time-out fast. How can we correct this? Simply stop disagreeing with one another? That's not going to happen—put twenty serious Christians in the same room, and they simply are not going to agree on everything. No, the only way is for us to emphasize what binds us together, not what drives us apart. Jesus tells us that he wants us to be a joyful people. "Joyful, Joyful, We Adore Thee" is not just the name of a song, it's a description of how the people of God should look. Joyful.

Jesus talked with his disciples about the joy he wanted them to have just before he was going to be crucified. Can you imagine that? Within hours after he talked to his disciples about joy, he was on his face before his Father in heaven, weeping and crying out because he saw so clearly the depths of the suffering he would endure.

But John 15 describes him, just hours before experiencing damnation for his people, talking to his disciples about the way they should love one another, even to the point of giving their lives for each other (vv. 5-17). The sheer depth of these few sentences is so enormous that those who love Christ spend their entire lives trying to understand them. If we love Christ, we remain in Christ, the vine. If we love Christ, his words become the center of our attention every day. If we love him, we obey him. If we love him, we will sacrifice for each other the way he sacrificed for us. If we love him, we will pray to the Father in his name, and we'll receive what we ask for.

All of this is supposed to make us joyful people. How could Jesus be talking about joy when he was so close to the cross's horror? Hebrews 12:2 gives the answer: "Let us fix our eyes on Jesus, the author and perfecter of our faith, who for the joy set before him endured the cross, scorning its shame, and sat down at the right hand of the throne of God."

As in everything in the Christian life, Jesus is our example, our pattern, our template. As he walked to the cross, totally committed to doing his Father's will, he moved toward a horror not just a little bit beyond what we can imagine, but a horror that was infinitely greater than the worst horror we can imagine. And as he moved toward that, he never wavered because he saw the joy beyond the cross.

Why are we not more joyful? Not hard to figure out. It's because we are not focused on the joy that is before us. We are not always thinking about our glorious destiny—the glory that Jesus died for so that we could share it with him. It is a glory so brilliant it was enough to sustain him and give him joy in the shadow of the cross.

If we were more joyful, would Bill's son be where he is today? What about all those sons and daughters out there who have left us because we fight so much? Would they be so far away from home if they could say, "I miss them, oh, I miss them. They were always so loving and so full of joy"?

Lord Jesus Christ, may we be so overwhelmed by the wonder of our future glory that all day today we may show others that we are joyful people. May those who have left us for whatever reason see our joy and return so that they can share this joy with us. Amen.

EIGHTY-TWO

When the Rubber Hits the Road

Whatever you do, work at it with all your heart,
as working for the Lord, not for men.
—Colossians 3:23

The trouble with being a Christian nowadays is that there are so many "Christian" things going on—things like worship services, church school classes, Bible study and prayer groups, evangelistic meetings, and conventions. Why, you can be busy all the time being a Christian! This is a problem because it obscures the fact that being a Christian is really about what you do the rest of the time—whether it's driving a CTA bus in Chicago, fork-lifting crates in a warehouse, mitering corners in a house, selling advertising, starting up a business or keeping one from crashing. It's in such situations that the rubber hits the road.

The Christian things that we do are important, and it's nice that we have so many. But when Christ and the Holy Spirit put the church together, they had something in mind in addition to singing "psalms and hymns and spiritual songs." They were thinking about a group of ordinary people who had been transformed by divine power, out there doing the things people do every day in the home and in the workplace, and doing them all while filled with the Holy Spirit.

Colossians 3 confronts us with a startling idea, which, sadly, many expressions of Christianity have missed. Great church buildings; religious functionaries all decked out in special robes carrying long staffs; Protestant, Catholic, and Orthodox rituals along with uncounted traditions, all give the impression that once we get out on the street we can breathe a sigh of relief and do as we please. That doesn't mean sin necessarily, but it does mean that out in the secular world, we live by different rules. It's almost a relief to get back to the office, where we can be ourselves.

No, the Bible says, it's not that way. Christ is watching all the time. This statement is addressed to slaves, of all people, slaves who sometimes worked for really cruel masters. Forget your masters, the Bible says, look at it this way—you are not working for those guys; you are working for an exalted master, Jesus Christ.

Practically this means, work hard. That's the first rule. Work with all your heart. How can God say this to us when everybody knows it's better to pray than to work? Isn't it? God is the great worker, the Master Builder of the universe. God is active, energetic, dynamic, and God created us in his image. We learn here that God doesn't like lethargy; God wants his followers to be people who do whatever their job happens to be enthusiastically. Some of us have manual jobs, menial jobs. We can transform these jobs into service done for Christ Jesus. Some of us have skills and professions. In that case, we should not be proud, but simply do our job as a service to the Lord Jesus. He has given us the gifts we need to do our jobs, and he wants us to dedicate every hour on the job to him.

Of course, what is addressed to first-century slaves in Colossians 3 also applies to us. Most of us have masters nowadays too. A worker pulling down a six-figure salary has a master: the person he works for owns him. We have bosses and foremen. Baseball players who are traded are slaves. Some slaves make more money than others, but most people work for someone. And it's not always pleasant doing so. In that case, we can tell ourselves, Jesus wants me to work hard and offer what I do to him, not to Bill Gates.

This also means, doesn't it, making sure that what we are doing is basically honest and worthwhile. Presiding over craps games for Donald Trump doesn't count—don't try to dedicate that to Christ. Running an escort service doesn't either. I think that Jesus would say to slaves who were pressed into work that was dishonest, sexually immoral, or inhumane, "You had better run away . . . and run as far away as you can."

What's exciting here is that the Bible tells us that if we truly believe in the Lord, the Lord wants us to turn an ordinary day at the bank into a worship service. Service = the work we do, and worship = dedicating our work to Christ. That's a worship service, isn't it?

When we worship like that all of the time, our worship of God in church becomes much more meaningful and beautiful.

Lord Jesus, it's so good to know that you are interested in the ordinary daily tasks we do. Teach us to worship you properly in church, but teach us to worship you properly too when we are on the job, where we spend most of our time. Amen.

EIGHTY-THREE

Pleasing the Spirit

The one who sows to please the Spirit, from the Spirit will reap eternal life.
—Galatians 6:8

One of the fascinating things about the Bible is that it frequently connects two things we would never expect to see together. In Galatians 6:7-10, for instance, we read about something so simple and obvious, it almost seems funny to write it down. It's this principle: you reap what you sow. Sow corn, reap corn—you don't have to be a neurosurgeon to figure that out. But in the same few sentences, we find out that it is possible to sow in such a way that we will be destroyed and another way so that we will live forever. The movement here from the obvious and common to the non-obvious and exalted is so quick it is almost stunning. Usually, though, when we read material like this, we are not stunned because we let it just slide past us.

The apostle Paul uses the obvious figure of speech here to alert us to the fact that we are always in the process of sowing something or another; the important consideration when it comes to sowing is who is pleased with what we are sowing. There are two possibilities. First, it is possible to please our sinful nature. Second, it is possible to please the Holy Spirit.

Our sinful nature is our nature as it is without the Holy Spirit. Unfortunately, a measurable residue of that nature remains even within those who actually do have the Spirit. In fact, the book of Galatians was written to Christians who had received the Holy Spirit, but who were reverting back to a form of religion that was about to scuttle them.

People please the sinful nature when they purposely follow a path that they know leads away from God rather than toward God. Sometimes Christians (yes, they are actually Christians) can become drunk with totally false ideas—like the man who convinces himself that it will be okay to leave his wife, or the woman, her husband. Christians like that know it's wrong, but somehow they convince themselves that it's right for them. They are pleasing the sinful nature. When we sow to please that nature, we will reap destruction—this spiritual law operates as automatically as the law of gravity.

On the other hand, we can sow to please the Spirit. People who know themselves to be forever people who are already living their eternal lives must think about this possibility all the time. Just think—it is possible for us, with all our weaknesses and leftover sinfulness, to please God, actually please God. And we do that when we please the Holy Spirit who lives within us.

The Bible portrays Christians as people who are living with God all the time, living with the Holy Spirit within them. It's not as if God is way out there somewhere, and we are stumbling around on this planet for a few decades, after which we will go to be with him. Instead, God is right here with us as we "stumble around," if we want to call it that. The Holy Spirit is within us, closer than close.

We must remember that whatever we do throughout the course of a day, we do in the presence of the Holy Spirit. And the Holy Spirit is either pleased with us or not. Ephesians 4:30 talks about grieving the Holy Spirit. The Holy Spirit is divine, the third person of the Holy Trinity, and it is possible to grieve him. How? Bitterness, rage and anger, slandering other people, malicious thoughts and actions will do it (4:31). When we act like that, we make the Holy Spirit very sad.

But we can also please him. This is a remarkable idea, really. The other day, a dear friend of mine said, "God must be easy to please. If he weren't, we could never do it." I had never thought about that before. I assumed that we poor sinners were displeasing him all the time. Not necessarily. It is also possible to please the Holy Spirit. Here's one way: "Be kind and compassionate to one another, forgiving each other, just as in Christ God forgave you" (4:32)

The Holy Spirit, whom we can please, is the very person who makes it possible for us to please him. Galatians 6 makes it very clear: if we try to please our own nature (which is sinful), the result will be destruction. If we try to please the Holy Spirit, who is also the Holy enabler, we will reap eternal life.

It's a great joy to be a Christian, living eternal life even now.

Holy Spirit, help us remember that you will be walking beside us each step of the way today. Give us your power so that we will sow to please you. Keep us from sin and show us how to live for you, no matter what happens. For Jesus' sake, Amen.

EIGHTY-FOUR

Gentlemen

But the fruit of the Spirit is . . . gentleness. . . .
—Galatians 5:23

I probably should, but I do not read Miss Manners very often. When I do, I am always impressed with the way she addresses people like me as "gentle reader." It's sort of heartwarming to have someone consider you a gentle person. Gentle people are rare.

Gentleness, as a desired characteristic, is not high on the charts. Those who mention that they are gentle when filling out a job application could well be passed over. Personnel managers are looking for aggressive people who will stop at nothing to get the job done. Gentleness does not fit in.

Unfortunately, even within the church gentleness is not considered a terribly important virtue. To be sure, there are people who demonstrate gentleness, but when it comes to leadership within the church—and leadership is a big thing nowadays—gentleness is not considered the priority characteristic. Church boards figure that they need a driver as the CEO of their church. Gentleness is a quality that can be held against people.

One of the great needs of the church these days is to refocus on gentleness. *"Re-focus"* isn't really the right word—most of us have to focus on it for the first time. But just think what our lives would be if we were gentle people. Many marriages would be a lot different, many household situations would be, and many churches would bring more glory to God. Denominations too would profit if high-level meetings were to open with a prayer imploring God to make people gentle.

Even as you read this, I am sure you assume that this is really very impractical. But honestly, is the other way practical? I mean the way we ordinarily live—making sure our rights are not violated, making sure our ideas are taken into consideration, making sure the people around us treat us properly—is this working?

I have been in meetings of church leaders that were exceedingly unpleasant. I remember one in which a man picked up his things and stalked out of the room in anger. The others sat in stunned silence until someone ventured the timorous remark, "If he's going to be in heaven, I don't want to be there." It was an evil moment, and we desperately needed some gentleness in that room.

The reason we have such a low evaluation of gentleness is that there isn't much we can do to acquire it and maintain it in our own lives. The Bible calls gentleness one of a number of virtues that are together the fruit of the Holy Spirit. The Holy Spirit has to move in and take control of our lives before we can be gentle.

The Holy Spirit creates gentleness and sustains it in believers' lives as he turns their attention toward the Lord Jesus Christ. The word that is translated as "gentleness" in the New International Version is consistently translated as "meekness" in the King James Version. Jesus uses the same word when he says, "Blessed are the *meek,* for they will inherit the earth." And gentleness is ascribed to Christ in connection with his meekness; the apostle Paul says, "By the meekness and the gentleness of Christ, I appeal to you" (2 Cor. 10:1). In that instance, even in the NIV, the word for "meekness" is the same as the word translated "gentleness" in Galatians 6. (And the word translated as "gentleness" is actually another word.) The point is just this: Jesus is the truly gentle person. When he took upon himself his lowly station, he conducted himself accordingly. He was the gentleman par excellence.

The Holy Spirit gives us gentleness as we look to Jesus. As we observe him and listen to him speaking, we learn what gentleness is. To be sure, sometimes his words were harsh, especially when he was in open conflict with the forces of darkness, but his overall demeanor was gentleness.

Gentleness comes from looking at Jesus and recognizing that, just as he humbled himself and took the form of a servant, so we who follow him must do the same. This is life eternal: to look at Jesus Christ and to want to be like him. This is life eternal: to look at Jesus Christ and to implore the Holy Spirit to come into our life and make us like Christ.

Everything would look different if God's people would earnestly try to be gentlemen and gentlewomen. So, gentle reader, why not pray this prayer from your gentle heart?

Holy Spirit, turn my eyes on Jesus Christ. Please make him the central person in my life. As you gave him the power to be gentle, even when he knew the harshness of the conflict with darkness, so give me a gentle spirit in this day. For Christ's sake, Amen.

EIGHTY-FIVE

My Amaryllis

Not even Solomon in all his splendor was dressed like one of these.
—Matthew 6:29

"Little man," God said, "I want to show you something."
It was late at night, and I was about to call it a day. I walked by the entrance to our dining room and stopped, surprised by what had happened to the amaryllis.

Someone had graciously given us the plant just before Christmas; the rough, large bulb just broke the surface of its pot. During the weeks prior to Christmas I had noticed the plant grow ever taller, a pale green stalk thrusting a large bud higher and higher until it reached twenty-seven inches. I must say that the plant looked rather odd to me, the single stalk, bending grotesquely toward the light with no flower to justify all the fuss it was making as it reached for the sky. Sometimes we would turn the pot to get the stalk pointing straight up once again. Obediently, it would make a correction, so that, by the time the flower appeared, it was plumb.

The Christmas season is a busy one, of course, and the amaryllis prepared for its glory unnoticed. But when the flowers finally burst the bud, we set it in the dining room where we could see it more. And see it I did, but look at it I did not, until that late evening something drew me to this Christmas lily.

I was stunned.

I could not believe my eyes. There were six perfectly formed flowers arranged in a circle, crowded together in the umbel, the terminal cluster. Each perianth, each funnel-shaped flower was blush with a light rose color arranged in delicate lines coming from the center, with the lower third of each flower pristine white. Some of the petals of the flowers had a small scalloped section that turned upward. And the long pistils turned downward from the center of each flower, six of them with a light yellow stamen, and one, longer than the others, with a stamen of deep maroon. These feeble words are like ash compared to the striking beauty of that stately plant.

I am not one who claims to hear the voice of God saying this and saying that, but that magnificent creation of the Lord was like a message from the heart of God himself. The creation, we are told, conveys a wordless message regarding God's power and divinity.

There are times when we cannot escape that message, times when the clouds lift across a snowcapped mountain range and we are startled by their majesty. But the message from the amaryllis is God's still, small voice, almost taunting us, reminding us that human artistry cannot come close to the beauty God has made. A flower is just there, often unnoticed. No thunder arises from within it to call our attention to its wonder; it is just there, and usually people like me stride right past on our way to important dates with destiny.

How many are the forests filled with beauty never noticed by human beings like ourselves? How many are the jungle flowers that burst with color never seen by any person? What does the amaryllis say? We cannot transcribe its message, for it speaks no words. But when we look at its beauty, it is as if God joins his heart to ours. We hear God whisper, "Don't say anything, just gaze and remember that the delicate hues of blush red and the petals with their scalloped edges are telling you that I am the God of beautiful things. In heaven you will forever be enthralled by what you see."

Many years ago, the creator of all this stood with his disciples in a field resplendent with lilies something like my amaryllis. He reminded them that Solomon, in all his splendor, didn't come close to the beauty of the lilies of the field. And Jesus told his disciples that whenever they looked closely at the lilies, they should remember that God would always take care of them. "If that is how God clothes the grass of the field, which is here today and tomorrow is thrown into the fire, will he not much more clothe you, O you of little faith?" (Matt. 6:30).

Yes, we are people of little faith, sad to say. Our anxiety knows no bounds. There are many reasons for this, some of them perfectly understandable, others not. Possibly one of the greatest reasons we are so often in a dither and distressed is that we do not notice what God puts right before our eyes. We stride right past and never see the beauty of the flowers. And so we never receive the wordless message from the heart of God.

Heavenly Father, gently lead us to those precious places where we can receive a message that will replace the trouble in our hearts with the wonderment of beauty and the assurance of your perfect care for us each day. In Christ, Amen.

EIGHTY-SIX

Counterfeit Miracles

The coming of the lawless one will [display] all kinds
of counterfeit miracles, signs and wonders.
—2 Thessalonians 2:9

E ver since she left the meeting, she has been looking for the man in the red flannel shirt sitting on the chair with the black leather seat. Some days she forgets about him entirely, but then there are days when she wonders if she might possibly find him. One thing she knows: the moment she sees him, she'll turn and flee. The preacher had told her, "Under no circumstances are you to leave with that man."

But was he a preacher? That was the question that haunted her. That is, was he a truly bona fide preacher of the gospel, or was he something else, a representative of dark powers? He had held his listeners spellbound as he made many of the statements you'd expect preachers to make. But then he had moved away from his preaching and had begun to relate strangely to those who were there. He'd chosen certain ones to "minister" to. He would then tell those he had chosen things about themselves that were true but that he had no way of knowing, except . . . except through some kind of supernatural revelation. People were stunned by what he'd said about them. And then he would say something about their future, about what was going to happen to them.

She had felt very uneasy when he confronted her and asked if he might minister to her. When she consented, he told her about what was going on in her life at that moment. She trembled inside as he told her about events he had no way of knowing, except . . . except . . . And then he told her that she would meet the man in the red flannel shirt; she would see him sitting on a chair with a black leather seat. And he warned her to have nothing to do with him.

Since then, she has lived in dread that she might see him, possibly in a bus station, possibly in a restaurant, possibly at some public event, possibly even in church. She sometimes glances furtively to the right and left, wondering if he might be there on the periphery of her vision. If only she could forget about him. She especially wants to forget the man because she has come to the conclusion that the one who had told her about the chair and the man sitting in it was not a bona fide preacher of he gospel.

Yes, the service had had the trappings of a regular Christian worship service. But after a fairly ordinary beginning, it had changed. It had gone on and on and on . . . literally for hours. And what was he doing, she'd wondered—did anything in the Bible support the notion that the Holy Spirit is busy frightening college girls about strange men in their futures? The man, apparently, was actually a psychic masquerading as a preacher, manipulating the people who were there.

The young woman I'm telling you about is a serious Christian who wants nothing more than to be in the will of God. This is the way it is for those who know that they belong to Christ, and they are on their way to meet him. She is a seeker, and that's why she went to the meeting in the first place. But when she left, she felt emotions she had never felt before, and she was confused and upset. Deeply religious people who love God and Christ and who want to do what is right are in danger because it is so easy for them to go down a track that will hurt them rather than help them.

There is such a thing as a counterfeit miracle, something we cannot explain. Exodus 7:11 reports that when Aaron threw down his rod and it became a snake, the Egyptian sorcerers did the same. And the apostle Paul tells the church in Thessalonica that "the coming of the lawless one will be in accordance with the work of Satan displayed in all kinds of counterfeit miracles, signs and wonders, and in every sort of evil that deceives those who are perishing" (2 Thess. 2:9-10).

That's scary. We must be careful. It's easy to get sucked into something that looks like it will be spiritually helpful and find out that it is just the opposite. The apostle Paul describes "deceitful workmen masquerading as apostles of Christ." Then he adds, "No wonder, for Satan himself masquerades as an angel of light. It is not surprising, then, if his servants masquerade as servants of righteousness" (2 Cor. 11:13-15).

Holy Spirit, give us discernment so that we will not be led astray
by the deceitfulness of those who masquerade as apostles but who
are not. Deliver us from anything that has anything to do with
the false spirits who oppose your kingdom. Amen.

EIGHTY-SEVEN

The Battle of the Red Dragon

The great dragon was hurled down—
that ancient serpent called the devil, or Satan.
—Revelation 12:9

Sometimes those who know they are on the way to glory have several days in a row in which they feel positively balmy about their lives. They feel good, their children are doing well at the moment, they are doing well on the job, and their investments aren't doing too badly either, thank you. Such interludes, for interludes they are, can lull a person into thinking that everything is hunky-dory; yes, I do think I'll have some ice cream on my apple pie.

But there are other times when the overpowering fury of evil hits us like a ton of bricks; there is just no escaping the fact that forces abroad in our land, in our very lives, are bent on destroying us. This can happen when we feel the merciless brunt of American-style persecution, which differs from Chinese but is real nevertheless. It can happen when someone dear to us goes off on her personal revolt against heaven. It can happen when something we see on television or stumble over on the Internet shows us how perverse our age has become. And it can happen when an incident reveals that evil does not start outside our skin but is well-established within us.

When we reel back in dismay and frantically seek an effective response to the pervasiveness of evil, we should understand that, as children of our heavenly Father, we are always involved in a battle that cannot be described in simple, earthly terms. Revelation 12 tells about that battle. It's a chapter that contains a description of conditions on earth right now; it's not about the future.

We discover that the origin of the overpowering evil that relentlessly confronts us is in heaven, a realm that existed before creation and that shall continue even after earth has been purified by fire. Evil has come by way of the flying red dragon who dominates Revelation 12. His other names are "the serpent" and—let's be honest—Satan.

Before the serpent sidled up to Eve in paradise, there had been a terrific battle in heaven: "Michael and his angels fought against the dragon, and the dragon and his angels fought back. But he was not strong enough, and they lost their place in heaven" (vv. 7-8). It was this battle and the expulsion that followed that led to the entrance of evil into the place we live. To be sure, evil would not have established its stranglehold on our planet if we had not cooperated, but the great conflict had begun before we did that, when the archangel Michael mobilized the righteous hosts of angels and defeated Satan and his wicked regiments.

So it was a defeated army, headed by a general who sought another way to topple the true God, that took over this place to begin with. And the events we now observe as this conflict continues to rage are fundamentally spiritual. Those were spiritual beings that attacked the triune God and his angels in heaven, and all the horror of the material manifestations of the battle must not make us forget that we are observing something spiritual—the continuation of the battle that began when Michael met the enemy and prevailed.

What this means is that evil can never be overestimated. The flying red dragon of Revelation 12 and all the angels he has enlisted in his service are totally ruthless. They will stop at nothing to destroy those who belong to Christ. It is foolhardy for believers to assume that they can play with evil ideas and evil things and escape unscathed.

Yes, there are days when the reality of this battle seems to recede, giving us a brief respite from the struggle. But the struggle will not be completed during our lifetime. Let us enjoy the occasional times of relative peace and exalted spiritual experience that can occur, but let us not allow anything to lull us to sleep.

Given the ferocious character of our horrible enemy, we must never be complacent. Our enemy has been beaten in heaven; this is his last chance to establish a kingdom in the universe. He will stop at nothing to succeed. We must stop at nothing to oppose him.

O warrior Lord, you who have gone forth to do battle with the enemy of heaven, be now our armorer. Clothe us with the impenetrable armor that will protect us, and equip us as we advance to meet Michael's enemy and ours. We pray for your name's sake, Amen.

EIGHTY-EIGHT

Swallowing Herring

We . . . wish . . . to be clothed with our heavenly dwelling,
so that what is mortal may be swallowed up by life.
—2 Corinthians 5:4

The images we usually associate with death make our skin crawl and our eyes fill with tears—shootings litter our streets with the dead on Saturday nights and leave blood on the library floor at school.

And even when we try to make death look good, we still hate it. I think of a woman I prayed with in the waiting room of a funeral home because she would not go into the room where her brother's body lay. I think of sons who refused to look at their father in the casket; nothing could persuade them. Understandable.

We need some new images when we think about death, especially when we think about our own. Here's one: *swallow.* The old King James Version of the Bible uses it in 2 Corinthians 5:4, and other translations use it too. It's just right. The Bible says that when believers die, their mortality is swallowed up by life.

Most of the swallowing we do is so automatic we never think about it. All we know is that when we swallow something, it disappears; it's taken into our system and transformed into something else. But sometimes swallowing can be more dramatic.

In the Netherlands, when the new herring come in, it's good to buy them fresh from the sea, raw and succulent. They lie there invitingly on the vendor's cart, heads off, gutted. Some people love to take those new herring by the tail, tilt their heads way back, and swallow them whole. They are soooo good. Delicious. Others are appalled and turn away in disgust. But for connoisseurs, this gift from the sea is very special.

In any case, this dramatic form of swallowing allows us to sense the wonderful meaning of 2 Corinthians 5:4. Ultimately, it is the fate of death itself to be swallowed up by life. Some day, life is going to swallow death. That will surely happen for anyone who loves Jesus, the prince of life. When a believer dies, we sometimes say that the person has left the land of the dying and entered the land of the living. People who hear that for the first time may be startled for a few moments, but then they will understand and nod their heads and agree that yes, of course it's true, even though it's not the way we usually think about death. But it's the way believers should always think about death. For those who love Christ, all that is mortal will be swallowed up by life the day they die.

It is very hard to truly live and think this way. Usually the ordinary ways of thinking about death intrude. It's the only way we know. We are prisoners of our habits when it comes to thinking about death. How can we break these bad habits and think about death as the time when life swallows death up once and for all?

We can start by looking at ourselves. In 2 Corinthians 5, we learn that "God has made us for this very purpose and has given us the Spirit as a deposit, guaranteeing what is to come" (v. 5). So when we talk about life swallowing death, we are not expressing a comforting fantasy; we are acknowledging the divine purpose for human life. God created us for life, and after we chose sin and death instead, God did everything that had to be done in order to override the enormous harm we caused. He did the ultimate to correct the hideous threat that humanity introduced into God's sinless world.

Now God has given us his very self in the person of the Holy Spirit who lives within us. There are many evidences of his presence, starting with faith. Who would believe the sacred Scriptures if it were not for the Holy Spirit within? It is the Holy Spirit who enables us to trust in Christ for our salvation, and it is the Holy Spirit who implants within us the sense of immortality we cannot escape.

The death that still clings to believers, refusing to let them go, will one day be swallowed up by life, inextinguishable life. Unbelievers may say, "What nonsense!" But believers respond, "Yes it is, in a way, but the very Spirit-created certainty I have is proof that it will surely be." The very Holy Spirit who assures us that death will be swallowed up by life is the guarantee that this is surely so.

Almighty God, drill the certainty of my eternal life into my heart so that nothing can dislodge it. Use my assurance that I am moving toward the swallowing up of my mortality to give me courage and joy. Holy Spirit, do not abandon me, I pray. For Jesus' sake, Amen.

EIGHTY-NINE

The Glory Road

Our present sufferings are not worth comparing with the glory . . .
—Romans 8:18

F ran is plucky. When she can, she forces herself out of bed and spends as much time as possible in her wheelchair. Her oxygen hose is long enough to give her some range. She dislikes lying in her bed, groggy in la-la land because of the morphine. In heaven, Jesus is putting the finishing touches on her room; once that's all taken care of, she won't have to stay in Room 425 anymore. But meanwhile, she's waiting, and sometimes, when the pain becomes too intense, she has to let the morphine take over. This is what she gets for refusing treatment for her cancer.

A couple of years ago, she had the choice to go the chemo route or let the enemy take her down. Her age and what she knew about the side effects of treatment made her say thanks but no thanks. She knew a lot about God and about prayer; she knew that God would help her handle the results of her choice.

But suffering is suffering, and there's usually a stretch of it in most people's lives, often near the end. Mirth Vos, who wrote about her anguish as she thought about leaving her family because of her cancer in *Letters to Myself on Dying*, remarked that living with the pain and the anxiety was "shadow of death" living. Most people, she said, are called upon to do a chunk of this type of living. Fran was doing her chunk.

"Well," says the apostle Paul, "Let me let you in on a secret: what you're going through is not worth comparing with the glory . . ." "Glory?" people ask when they live tethered to an oxygen hose, ramping up the morphine when they need it. "What do you mean, glory?"

What Paul writes in Romans 8:18 is fascinating: "I consider that our present sufferings are not worth comparing with the glory that will be revealed in us." He does not say here that we are on a journey toward a glorious place that will make us forget the place of suffering, in the same way as going shopping will make you forget your arthritis. No, he says that glory will be revealed *in us*. "For those God fore-knew he also predestined to be conformed to the likeness of his Son, that he might be the firstborn among many brothers. And those he predestined, he also called; those he called, he also justified; those he justified, he also glorified" (vv. 29-30).

Sometimes when we visit people like Fran who have lived many decades, raised their children and embraced their grandchildren, we come away shaking our heads and muttering about how depressing it is to grow old. We see a woman shrunken to a wisp of her former self, skin and bones, large blue-black blotches on her hands and arms, and we wonder if God hasn't miscalculated—does this really have to hap-pen? We need to remind ourselves that people like Fran who trust in Jesus are on the verge of being glorified—not just entering into glory but being glorified, which is what Paul was talking about when he talked about the glory that will be revealed *in us*.

Life is a glory road—for believers in Christ, it is a road to glory. Who says? Paul says, and Paul knows. He is one of the few people who have seen what glory looks like. Once, as Paul traveled to destroy Christ, Christ destroyed him by appearing to him in his startling splendor. Three times the book of Acts records the glorified Christ's unique meeting with this brutal Christ-hater. That encounter changed Paul from inside out. Christ's glory was revealed in him.

Paul also records a mysterious event, which he describes in subdued, even puz-zling terms in 2 Corinthians 12:2-7, that makes his description of the glorified experience of believers credible. He tells about a man who was caught up into para-dise, where he "heard inexpressible things, things that a man is not permitted to tell." He calls what happened then "surpassingly great revelations."

So when Paul talks about glory and glorification, he's not talking through his hat.

We will be glorified. Fran knew that she would be. She was very eager. We should be too—all the time, not only when the end comes, but every day. Often we are called to carry a cruel burden. Often our days are unspeakably harsh. We have to keep our shining destination in mind always.

Glory is going to be revealed in us. In us! We are going to be transformed so that we will be glorified with the same glory that is in Christ.

Lord Jesus, we are thankful that you give us sisters and brothers
who show us how to suffer with glory always in mind. Help us
always to remember the glory that will make whatever we suffer
seem as nothing in comparison. In your name, Amen.

NINETY

Meanwhile, Back on Planet Earth

Whom have I in heaven but you? And earth has nothing I desire besides you.
—Psalm 73:25

I t is good to be forever people and to know that our lives are already preparation for eternity. For believers, eternal life is now, and just remembering that can be an inspiration.

But most of us are not like the thief on the cross, who believed in Jesus as his savior and within hours entered into paradise. Most of us live for several decades here on planet earth, and sometimes what we see here is very depressing.

Psalm 73 is a realistic expression of what it's like to have great expectations for eternity while we live in a depressing world where it often appears as if God isn't paying much attention to what is going on. The writer notes that unbelievers often make a mint, while people like him don't do well at all.

It's interesting that the writer of this ancient psalm is on the same wavelength we are today. Judgments about others are made in terms of how rich they become. Even the venerable prophet Jeremiah looked at other people that way. "Why does the way of the wicked prosper?" he asked. "Why do all the faithless live at ease?" (Jer. 12:1).

The question persists. Why, pray tell, do those who don't seem to care much about God cruise on the Sky Deck, in a deluxe suite? These people don't care anything about God. A lot of these wicked people will say very spiritual things sometimes. "Their mouths lay claim to heaven, and their tongues take possession of the earth. . . . This is what the wicked are like—always carefree, they increase in wealth" (vv. 9, 12).

And then the psalmist bemoans his own sad fate. His is a grim litany of bad deals and failure, even though he loves God and wants to follow him. There is nothing subtle about this psalm—it's a plain old pity party, and the person who wrote it wants God to hear every word.

Then something happens. We don't know exactly what, but it happens in God's house. Suddenly all of the writer's gloom dissolves before a vision of the greatness and kindness of God that surrounds him with love daily and forever cares for him.

On the one hand, he sees that the prosperity of the wicked is temporary because they do not enjoy the favor of God. Therefore, the day will come soon when they will experience God's wrath: "As a dream when one awakes, so when you arise, O Lord, you will despise them as fantasies" (v. 20). And he sees how totally stupid he had been when he bemoaned his own fate and wondered if God had forgotten him: "When my heart was grieved and my spirit embittered, I was senseless and ignorant; I was a brute beast before you" (vv. 21-22).

It was as if the mighty light of a rising sun drove away the blinding fog that had driven this man to his foolish lament. He realized that God was with him, and what more could he want while he lived in this world? He realized, as all who sense the presence of God in their lives realize, that this presence of God would never be cut off. Never.

"I am always with you; you hold me by my right hand. You guide me with your counsel, and afterward you will take me into glory. Whom have I in heaven but you? And earth has nothing I desire besides you."

We do not fall easily into this joy. While we live here, we all cast our jealous eyes right and left and see that wicked people prosper. We marvel at their wealth, their stretch limos, their private jets, their fabulous homes. And their power—when they walk into a room everyone caters to them, and when they speak, everyone listens. Christian people usually do not attain such wealth. We know that all this wealth will be left behind, but, human nature being what it is, we are impressed.

Blessed are those who understand that the greatest wealth is to be possessed by God. God is with us now. God will be with us then. Suddenly the clouds part. The sunlight of his good grace fills our little lives, and our confusion begins to dissipate.

If the writer of Psalm 73 discovered that, many centuries before God appeared to us in Christ his Son, how much more shouldn't we be thrilled to know that Christ, who holds our souls in this life, will receive us in the glory that will surely come?

What more could we want?

*O Lord, forgive our foolish ways. Help us understand that knowing
you and experiencing your grace provides us riches beyond compare.
Now we may have Jesus always. We hear him say, "I am with you always."
Jesus, ever with us stay, and bring us into your glorious presence. Amen.*

NINETY-ONE

Pleasure Seekers, Pleasure Finders

You will fill me with joy in your presence, with eternal pleasures at your right hand.
—Psalm 16:11

O ne of the defining differences between godless people and godly people is that godless people pursue pleasure and godly people don't. Well, if that's the case, godly people will have to change their thinking.

The destiny of the godly is joy and pleasure. Psalm 16 is very open about this. This Davidic psalm not only had a powerful impact when it was first written but also later, when Peter quoted it on Pentecost and connected it with Christ's resurrection. Peter explained to the crowd at Pentecost that the psalmist's declaration "You will not abandon me to the grave, nor will you let your Holy One see decay" did not actually refer to David at all. He reminded them that David actually did die and was buried, and he decayed. What he said actually referred to Jesus of Nazareth, who died and rose again and sent his Holy Spirit into his church.

This psalm, then, is extremely important for us today. It helps us discover that the destiny of serious, God-fearing people includes joy and even pleasures.

The truth is that all human beings are pleasure-seekers, even serious, God-fearing people, though we may be reluctant to admit it. Pleasure is, very simply, that which pleases us. Unpleasant things and events distress us. We avoid them.

Take a backache for example. Even those of us who are serious believers seek help when we are incapacitated by severe back pain. We carefully avoid anything that brings illicit pleasure, and we may even be very careful about enjoying too much of the ordinary pleasures, but when something ruins our well-being, we head for the nearest physician or chiropractor to get relief.

We often think of the Puritans as people who were opposed to pleasure on principle. But recent studies of their lives, and even of their poetry, reveal that many Puritan husbands had great affection for their wives, and they and their wives enjoyed the high pleasures of marriage together.

In reality, much of our behavior consists of pleasure-seeking in one form or another. Some people who have no faith seem to be almost frantically determined to achieve pleasure at any cost; they risk their health, their marriages, their families, their reputations, and their jobs, in some cases, for a brief time of intense pleasure. But deep down within themselves, those who take enormous risks to achieve destructive pleasure long for idyllic pleasure, which continues to escape them.

The desire for pleasure is in our bones. It's part of who we are. Because we do not always achieve it, we are often miserable and upset. Sometimes people are miserable without knowing what it is that is troubling them. We do not realize that what we need is a pleasure that goes beyond what we ordinarily think of as pleasure. We need the pleasure believers will realize in the presence of God.

If we would be continually conscious of the joy and pleasure that God has for us in the future, and which we have already begun to experience, our lives would be so much different from what they are. We try so frantically to achieve pleasures by our own means and on our own terms. And all the while God is surely telling us, "Take it easy, you will have joy and pleasure beyond imagining."

Praise God, those who trust in him already experience this reality in this world. Along with David, we can say, "The boundary lines have fallen for me in pleasant places; surely I have a delightful inheritance" (v. 6).

What could ever give us joy and pleasure so full and so enduring? Psalm 16 is very clear as it answers this question: God, and God alone, provides exactly what we need. The pleasures we will experience are going to be realized at the right hand of God. Only Christ will occupy the right hand of rulership, but we will be so close to Christ eternally that we will be at God's right hand too. We will be in the presence of God forever. This is why our joy and eternal pleasures will be without limit.

We who call ourselves forever people often pride ourselves with our seriousness, our dedication to accomplishing the work of the Lord. That's understandable. But deep down we need to know and realize that some day our mouths are going to be full of laughter and our hearts full of joy without ceasing; we will never have to stop our celebration to wipe a grief-tear from our eyes.

Lord Jesus, we are not accustomed to thinking about our future in this way. We are much too solemn most of the time. Startle us with the anticipation of eternal pleasure and help us live today with joy inside . . . and outside. Amen.

NINETY-TWO

How We Know

We know that we have passed from death to life, because we love our brothers.
—1 John 3:14

O ne of the most difficult things about having cancer is the strange relationship you have with time. Once you have been diagnosed and treated, only
time will tell whether the treatment has been successful. Five is usually the
magic number. Five years free, you can figure it's finished.

It's the numbers that give cancer survivors this peculiar relationship to time. On
the one hand, they want the years to go fast so that they can know they are cured.
On the other hand, if their cancer is going to come back in two years, or three, they
want the time to go slowly, so they can enjoy life and savor it.

What's the number of years it takes to know for sure if you are saved? Some
Christians say you can never know unless you have some kind of special revelation.
The apostle John wouldn't agree. He writes, "We know that we have passed from
death to life, because we love our brothers." It doesn't take years to know for sure
that you are saved; it just takes attitude.

Right here is something I don't like about the Bible: it makes statements that are
straightforward—no fudging, no qualifications, just, This is the way it is; take it or
leave it. This is one of those statements. If you really want to know if you are saved,
the Bible says, look inside your heart, and ask if you love your brother.

Who is John talking about here?

Most likely he is talking about loving fellow church members, both men and
women. And that's not always easy. If you are a church member, ask yourself this
question: Is there any person—possibly even several persons—in my church whom
I really don't care about very much? Or take it one step further: Is there anyone in

my church—or even several—whom I actively dislike? Are there people whom I deliberately avoid . . . right in my own church?

It happens. Yes, people who are part of the same church can become enemies. Have they passed from death into life if they don't get along? If they dislike each other? If they hate each other?

Come now, you may ask, is this really true? Must we love all of our brothers, no matter what? Yes, we should. But some of them are so unlovable, you say. And some of them have actually said things about me and done things to me and my reputation that pained me terribly, and I just cannot forget their behavior. How can I love such people? Is it really fair to make our love for brothers and sisters the litmus test when we try to figure out if we are truly saved?

God does this because love is what Christianity is all about. It's not about liturgy, it's not even about doctrine or prayer and Bible reading, it's about love. To be sure, each of these items has a role to play in the Christian faith. But there are millions of believers over the centuries who knew nothing about doctrine, who never owned a Bible, and who seldom, if ever, went to church because they didn't have one, but they passed from death into life. They believed that God loved them so much that he sent his one and only Son to be their Savior, and consequently they loved others who loved Jesus.

The apostle John also puts it this way: "God is love. Whoever lives in love lives in God, and God in him. In this way, love is made complete among us so that we will have confidence on the day of judgment" (1 John 4:16-17). Notice here again the connection between our love and the judgment. Sort of makes you shiver, doesn't it?

The reason there is such a close tie between our love and our salvation is this: If we don't love those who are closest to us, those whom Jesus has loved enough to die for, apparently we haven't really understood how magnificent Christ's love for us is. If Jesus Christ died for me while I was still a sinner, how can I refuse to love someone who is my brother or my sister? How can I retain a bitter spirit? How can I nurse a grudge? How can I refuse to forgive when I have been forgiven so much?

Whenever I read 1 John 3:14, I can't help but shudder. Yes, it's as simple as this. The litmus test that tells me whether I have passed from death into life is whether or not I love. The same is true for everyone who reads this.

O loving Savior, destroy my bitterness, my critical spirit, my failure to forgive, and transform me into a loving person. Thank you for loving me enough to die on the cross for me. Don't let me ever forget what you have done for me. In your name, Amen.

NINETY-THREE

Airborne

After that, we who are still alive and are left will be
caught up together with them in the clouds. . . .
—1 Thessalonians 4:17

Whenever I read about the way we are going to meet Jesus in the air some-day, I realize that the Christian faith is a lot more than Bible study and theology. And it's more than what we do in church when we are together in worship. It's about soaring, taking off, being involved in events that taunt our imagination—we cannot even visualize what the Bible tells us is going to happen.

The believers in Thessalonica apparently had some worries they shouldn't have had. Paul had not been with them very long—maybe three sabbaths, maybe four, and that had not been enough time to clarify everything about Christ Jesus. Somehow the people had concluded that Christ was going to appear any minute now, and when some of their number died, they figured their dead friends and family would miss out on the excitement.

We can be thankful for their confusion, because it gave the apostle a chance to straighten things out for them . . . and for us. We also have lots of questions about what will happen when the end comes and Christ comes back.

When we read Paul's description of the role we are going to play when Christ returns, we realize that we need to discipline ourselves to think about biblical religion differently than we ordinarily do. Many of us learn it as children, and then we fit into the pattern of expected Christian behavior over the years. The realities revealed in the Bible actually become somewhat commonplace for us. Very likely, it's Satan himself who manages to get us to think about what we find in the Bible as if it were really not all that unusual.

And then we read 1 Thessalonians 4. It stuns us (if we actually think about what it means). We learn here that believers who have died will be summoned from heaven and reunited with their bodies, and then, in their resurrected bodies, they will rise to meet Christ. Believers who are alive at that time will then be raised to meet Christ in the air as well.

O Lord, you've got to be kidding!

No. No. This is really going to happen. The reason it puzzles us and leaves us about ready to drop back into an unbelieving mode is that we fail to realize that everything about our present state is incredible. Here we are, fragile children of dust, hurtling through space as part of a seemingly infinite universe, dependent each moment on oxygen from the air and nutrients from the soil, with all the intricate processes and balances that exist in our bodies, and we assume, we actually assume, that all this is happening because, well, this is just the way things are.

No. This is not just the way things are. God created the world this way in order to sustain us every moment and to keep us conscious of ourselves and of him. The substance of our bodies, the gravity that keeps us attached to the surface of this planet, the spatial relationships we automatically measure with our eyes are so much a part of our mental habits that we cannot conceive of reality without them. But the Bible tells us there is reality without these things.

The very same Creator through whom all this was made, Christ Jesus, is in total control of everything. And he will make it possible for our bodies to rise from the grave to be reunited with our souls so that we, complete once again, will be able to be part of Christ's new order of reality. We have no idea what this will be like, but we know that if he made the present order of reality so that it works, he can make any order of reality work.

As we read in 1 Thessalonians 4 about the rapture of God's people as they welcome the victorious Christ, we must tell one another and remind ourselves constantly that ultimately the Christian faith is about such mind-boggling reality.

It is already great *fun* to be a Christian while we are in this world. May I use that word? There is nothing in this world that compares with the joy and excitement that Christians can have. And it is going to be even more enjoyable to be part of what Christ does when he returns. Then we will be airborne.

Christ of the great victory, thank you for including us in the great events that will begin the new reality of the perfection of your kingdom. Forgive us for being so earthbound that we tend to treat 1 Thessalonians 4 as if it were fantasy. Please come quickly. Amen.

NINETY-FOUR

Will I Know Stephanie?

He looked up and saw Abraham . . . with Lazarus by his side.
—Luke 16:23

The question of whether we will know our loved ones in heaven becomes over-powering when someone you love with all your young heart is suddenly transferred from the realm of earth to the realm of heaven. For a young man I know who loved Stephanie and knew that he would marry her, that question was one of the first he asked when she fell to the ground and died on the way to an exam at college. Will I know Stephanie?

Yes, dear boy, you surely will.

The story Jesus told in Luke 16 about a certain rich man (often called Dives) and Lazarus, who continued to have contact with each other after they died, provides strong biblical proof that persons will recognize each other after death. But isn't this just a story? Yes, but would Christ Jesus, who knew firsthand the realities of heaven, have created a story that would give us false information?

Thankfully, the certainty we may have about knowing that we will recognize one another is not based on a single biblical sentence here and there. Our certainty is drawn from the Bible's total message.

Although Jesus' disciples did not recognize him when he appeared to them in his glorified body, Jesus did not allow them to continue in their awkward ignorance; he kept presenting himself until they knew who he was. (Read Luke 24:36-44 as an example.)

If we doubt that we will recognize other believers in heaven, we might well ask the question, Will I recognize myself? If we are not going to recognize each other, what makes us think that we will have any knowledge of our own identity?

Surely anyone who reads the Bible through several times will be struck by its emphasis on individual human beings. There is information in the Bible about more than 2,500 people, and many of them are described in detail. God himself appears in the Bible in human form; the Old Testament describes God as loving and hating and rejoicing and grieving and hearing and seeing. In the New Testament, the only true God appears to us as a human being who hungered and sweat and collapsed from fatigue. We call him Jesus of Nazareth.

In other words, the Bible is about persons, personality, individuality, identity, characteristics, idiosyncrasies—all of these appear on its pages as part of God's intentional creation of the human race as a variegated species in whom he derives great delight. The Bible tells us that each of us has been created by God's own hand within the womb. Our physical characteristics provide only a partial identity profile; other elements of that profile—emotional and intellectual characteristics—are also ours alone. We may be sure that the Almighty God who designed each one of us is not going to discard all that made us distinct individuals and turn us into a race of glorified Martians. We are God's imagebearers. We are unique. Each believer is an object of God's love. Stephanie will always be Stephanie, and those who knew her and loved her will love her forever and thank God for giving her to them.

The question of whether believers will know each other in heaven is extremely important, not only because an affirmative answer can help calm the troubled soul of the bereaved, but because our answer reveals how we view the connection between our present life and the life to come.

If believers are not going to recognize each other after death, and if they might not even know who they themselves are, this means that what happens after death will be an entirely new start. Everything that happens in this life will be scrapped. But nothing in the Bible supports that notion; everything in the Bible contradicts it. The information we learn from the Bible about the coming judgment, about God's gracious rewards, about the resurrection of the body reveals a connection between this life and forever.

So I can say to my grieving friend, Yes, you will know Stephanie in heaven, and she will know you, and you will know each other better than you ever did before. In fact, come to think of it, all of us are going to spend forever appreciating Christ's unspeakable grace in each of our precious lives. Hallelujah!

Lord Jesus, thank you that we may believe that we are going to continue after death. And thank you for making it possible for us to know our loved ones who trust you forever and ever. Amen.

NINETY-FIVE

The Schedule

Then I saw a great white throne and him who was seated on it.
—Revelation 20:11

I
f you want to know the time of Christ's coming, sorry, but the Bible disappoints. As Jesus himself put it, "It is not for you to know the times or dates the Father has set by his own authority" (Acts 1:7).

We can't know the time of Christ's return, but we can compile a schedule of events from biblical data. Let's start with what happens when believers die: they go to be with Christ. According to the apostle Paul, either believers are at home in the body and away from Christ or out of the body and with Christ (2 Cor. 5:1-10). When they are with the Lord, they experience glory. At that time their dead bodies deteriorate in the earth, in fire, or in the sea.

When Christ returns, there will be a resurrection of the bodies of both believers and unbelievers. Daniel 12:2 speaks of this, and Jesus himself said, "A time is coming when all who are in their graves will hear his voice and come out—those who have done good will rise to live, and those who have done evil will rise to be condemned" (John 5:28-29).

After this great general resurrection, all human beings will be gathered before the great white throne. Revelation 20 makes clear that every person who has ever lived and died will appear there; even the sea and Hades will give up their dead.

Jesus also describes the great white throne judgment: "When the Son of Man comes in his glory, and all the angels with him, he will sit on his throne in heavenly glory. All the nations will be gathered before him, and he will separate the people one from another as a shepherd separates the sheep from the goats" (Matt. 25:31-32).

The schedule, then, looks like this: we die, our souls go to glory, and our bodies decay or are destroyed in a catastrophic event or enter the sea. At the end of human history, Christ will return, and there will be a general resurrection of all the people who have ever lived. They will be gathered before the great white throne and will be judged in terms of the record in what Revelation calls the "book." It will be a judgment in terms of their deeds: "The dead were judged according to what they had done as recorded in the books" (Rev. 20:12).

This means that the time between physical death and the return of Christ is a time in which the souls of people continue to exist; they are conscious, well aware of where they are, well aware of Christ, and, I believe, well aware of each other. Those who do not go to heaven are well aware of their situation and in deep sorrow and torment because they know that they are lost, and it is their own fault. When the reunion of the soul and the body occurs, those who are saved enter into the fullness of glory, and those who are not saved enter into the fullness of condemnation. Both groups experience their lot to the full after they receive their bodies because, without their bodies, their capacities for experiencing glory or condemnation are less than when they have their bodies.

The apostle Paul also talks about the fact that all of us will appear before the great white throne, where we will be judged. In the same passage in which he mentions being "at home with the Lord" when we die, he says that all of us will be judged: "We must all appear before he judgment seat of Christ, that each one may receive what is due him for the things done while in the body, whether good or bad" (2 Cor. 5:10).

The Bible offers ample evidence to support this schedule. One thing is sure: every life is precious, every hour is precious, and we must use our lives wisely because we will be judged for what we do. Everyone is eternal and will live forever, either before the face of Jesus or in the horrible state of condemnation. This is why it is so terribly important that we trust in Christ—so that when we stand at the great white throne, we will hear our Savior say, "Come, you who are blessed by my Father; take your inheritance, the kingdom prepared for you since the creation of the world" (Matt. 25:34).

Lord Jesus Christ, our eyes are so glued on the things of this world that we seldom pause and consider what you have in store for us. Help us to believe that something like this schedule will indeed occur, and help us to live as those who understand that the Judge is standing at the door. Amen.

NINETY-SIX

God Will Not Forget

God is not unjust; he will not forget your work and the love
you have shown him as you have helped his people. . . .
—Hebrews 6:10

F ew books in the Bible are more detailed and explicit about the full effectiveness of the finished work of Jesus Christ than the book of Hebrews. In it we
learn of the perfection of what Christ did for us when he became the final
great high priest, who did not have to bring offerings for his own sin but instead
brought the perfect offering of his own person for the sins of his people.

But with all its emphasis on Christ's finished work, Hebrews also emphasizes the
importance of the works that we do in this world. Chapter 6 calls believers not even
to think about turning aside from the faith they have learned. The opening verses of
the chapter describe the very idea of believers falling away as preposterous and
horrible.

And then comes this striking statement: God will not forget the works of his
people (v. 10). The perfection of God includes both a memory and a "forgettery,"
which he controls carefully. We are thankful that God chooses to forget our sins, in
the sense that once we have been cleansed through Jesus' blood, God will no longer
deal with us in terms of our iniquity. But God also assures us that he will graciously
remember the good things we have done.

The good works described in Hebrews 6 are common enough. They are the ordinary good things that believers do for one another as they live together in fellowship with Christ. The writer describes these ordinary good works in the most
exalted terms: the good things that Christians do as they help each other in their
need, they do to God himself.

We see here a reflection of what Christ taught in Matthew 25—those who care for the poor and visit those in prison are in reality doing these things to Christ. Here Hebrews strikes the same note: deeds of love done for the good of God's children are done to God himself.

Why does God remember these good things? First of all, because they are actually works that God himself does through us. They are part of the "good works package" God has prepared for believers. God gives us our faith, and then God gives us the works of faith that we may do. The works we are privileged to do bear the stamp of divine design. In and of ourselves, we would engage in actions that are quite different.

But the writer of Hebrews also introduces the idea of justice here. As believers exert themselves in activities that are worthwhile and God-honoring, God takes note. For God to allow what we do to be simply swept into the cosmic dustbin, without taking any account of it, would be contrary to the justice and the righteousness that is the foundation of God's throne.

The section in Hebrews 6 that assures us that God remembers our works of love concludes with a reminder that the faith that saves is a faith that works; it is marvelously active in the things of God. Those who are saved, we read, "inherit what has been promised" through faith and patience. That is a curious combination. We are saved by faith alone. Yes. But it is faith that is expressed in patient steadfastness, as God's people do the works of love God has created for them.

It is true that when we come before the judgment seat of God we will say, "Nothing in my hands I bring, simply to the cross I cling." Yet God, who in his justice has made us righteous in Jesus, will also, in his justice, remember what we have done in the strength of his grace.

This means that we who have been saved have every reason to rely on God for our salvation and for the strength to serve God each day. Each day we live in this world is eternally important. Our just and righteous God notes everything we do. If we turn to Christ for our salvation, God will forget our sin and will remember our work of love as if we have done it unto God. In all this, God's glorious justice will be expressed.

Holy, merciful, and just God, thank you for the wonder of salvation that makes it possible for us to be saved from our sins. And thank you for giving us holy work to do. Make us willing to serve you every day. We do so only in your strength. In Christ, Amen.

NINETY-SEVEN

The Heavenly Printout

The dead were judged according to what they had done as recorded in the books.
—Revelation 20:12

For Christian believers who are overjoyed because they have been washed in the blood of the Lamb and forgiven, it can be somewhat jarring to learn that one day, when they stand at the great white throne, they will be judged according to a heavenly printout of their actions and their motives.

Jesus says that we will be judged for every careless word we utter (Matt. 12:36). And the apostle Paul speaks of the day when Christ Jesus "will bring to light what is hidden in darkness and will expose the motives of men's hearts" (1 Cor. 4:5).

Some people try to wriggle from beneath the biblical teaching about the great judgment at the end of time by declaring that it applies only to unbelievers. But Matthew 25, which tells about the King separating the sheep from the goats in terms of what they have done for the poor and the imprisoned, depicts both believers and unbelievers before the Judge.

And Paul writes to the believers in Corinth that "it is necessary for all of us to appear before the judicial seat of Christ so that we can receive back what is due us for the things done through our bodies, whether good or bad" (2 Cor. 5:10; my translation).

Revelation 20 itself describes those who stand before the great white throne as having come from the realm of death and from the sea. Surely these include all the dead, and believers are among the dead in the sea.

In the light of statements like these, it should be no surprise to learn that there are books in heaven that carry the record of our actions on earth. Being justified through Jesus' blood does not mean that what we do from day to day has no significance; it's not that we are saved, and that's that. God not only forgives us through Christ's blood, but God also gives us the Holy Spirit, who equips us to live for Christ. The parable of the talents (Matt. 25:14-30) shows how we will be judged for what we have done with what the King has given us.

Revelation 20 tells us that there are two books in heaven. One contains the record of our works; the other—the book of life—contains the confirmation of our salvation. All those whose names are written in the book of life will never perish. You may be sure that your name is included in that book if you repent of your sins, believe in Christ for your salvation, and then live in the obedience of faith. But those whose names are written in the Lamb's book will be judged by the contents of the other book as well. The word *book*, of course, is a figure of speech; it refers to the record of everything that you and I have ever done that exists in the divine consciousness.

People who know that they are going to live forever . . . and ever . . . and ever . . . find enormous motivation for holy living and the performance of good works in their realization that they are going to stand one day at the great white throne. The apostle Paul states specifically what the expectation of the day of judgment causes in believers' lives: "We make it our goal to please him, whether we are at home in the body or away from it" (2 Cor. 5:9).

There need be nothing in our striving to please God that arises from a frantic desire to earn our salvation; that has already been fully accomplished at Calvary. Our motivation arises from our understanding that we are eternal people who are able to begin living as eternal people while we are in this world. Jesus is our Savior, and we want to please him; we do not want to grieve him or the Holy Spirit. He is the center of our vision. Everything we do, everything we think, is noted by our Savior. And one day, it will be revealed for us to see and for him to see.

If we have done anything that pleases him, we will give him the glory for it because we could have done it only in the power of his Holy Spirit. And when we realize then just how sinful we have been—when the blindness that hid it from us while we were in this world falls away—we will see the wonder of our justification as we have never seen it before.

Oh, that will be a terrible day! Oh, that will be a happy day! Oh, that will be glory for you and me!

Living Christ, you alone are righteous. You alone are holy. And you alone are merciful. May the remembrance of the day of judgment not be lost in my life in this day, and may I live as one who will one day give an account. I pray because of Calvary, Amen.

NINETY-EIGHT

Pella Justice

Then I saw a great white throne and him who was seated on it.
—Revelation 20:11

O n a wonderfully warm late May evening thirty-four years ago, I addressed the graduating class of Pella Christian High School in Iowa—a stalwart and attractive collection of big, blond young people. After the festivities, I visited with some of the teachers and headed back to Des Moines about 11 o'clock. Five miles out of town, a conscientious police officer stopped me to tell me he was upset about how eager I was to get to Des Moines and gave me a ticket. He then instructed me to follow him back into town, where he brought me before a justice of the peace.

I was paraded through the justice's living room, where I saw one of girls who had graduated sitting with a young man who was obviously thrilled with her achievement. I was not thrilled with mine. When I noticed one of our church's hymnbooks on the piano, I thought I might be let off the hook. How foolish! The justice of the peace, who had apparently come out of a deep slumber, read the charge and asked if I pleaded guilty. I did. And then he did what he was supposed to do. I paid him the fine and left, utterly mortified.

I have often had a good laugh with my Pella friends over this experience. I broke the law and I paid for it, in money and in deep embarrassment. I bring this up just now because it relates to what the apostle John saw when he saw the great white throne and *him who sat upon it.*

Say what you will—when you are guilty, who you get for a judge makes all the difference in the world. Judges have discretionary powers; they can throw the book at you or they can be lenient. For us guilty sinners who trust in Christ for salvation, there is great joy in learning the identity of the person on the great white throne. It is none other than Jesus Christ.

Christ Jesus is the great judge. "The Father judges no one, but has entrusted all judgment to the Son. . . . He has given him authority to judge because he is the Son of Man" (John 5:22, 26). This means that all who trust in Christ for salvation will have the very person who died for them as judge on the Day of Days.

Among all the treasures we find in Romans 8 is Paul's assurance that those who are trusting Christ for their salvation now have nothing to fear when they stand before the great white throne. "If God is for us, who can be against us? He who did not spare his own Son, but gave him up for us all—how will he not also, along with him, graciously give us all things?" (vv. 31-32).

The apostle also reminds us that we are going to stand before a judge who is our friend in the absolute sense: "Who will bring any charge against those whom God has chosen? It is God who justifies. Who is he that condemns? Christ Jesus, who died—more than that, who was raised to life—is at the right hand of God and is also interceding for us" (vv. 33-34).

Think of it this way: when we stand before Christ with all of our sins, we will be looking into the eyes of the person who died for us, who rose again for us, and who never stops praying for us. It's like having your mother as your judge. Now, it's true that your mother knows better than anyone else what's wrong with you, but you can be sure that she's going to go easy when she announces the sentence.

But in another sense, it's different from having your mother as your judge. Christ Jesus our judge not only knows our sin, but he has also paid for our sin. So we will stand in front of him, entirely aware of our guilt, but he will assure us then, as he does now, "Fear not, your sins are forgiven. I paid for them when I died for you on the cross."

Someday each of us will meet the judge, no question about it. But if you and I believe in Christ Jesus as our Savior today, we can know already that he has taken our punishment upon his own body on the cross. And he prays for us every day. What a friend we have in Jesus!

Lord Jesus Christ, we are thankful that you will be the one to judge us. Help us now to believe in you fully and to confess our sins. Take our fear and embarrassment away as we think of what it will be like to appear before you. Your blood saves us; your resurrected life equips us; your constant prayers assure us of your mercy. We praise you, Jesus. Amen.

NINETY-NINE

Finishing Strong

To him who is able to keep you from falling . . .
be glory, majesty, power and authority. . . .
—Jude 24-25

Several years ago, flying back from Russia with several others who had been in meetings with many high-level Soviet leaders, I sat back and mused about life with a publisher who had been in the meetings too. In a few years he would be retiring after an illustrious career, and he was feeling some misgivings. He said, "The one thing I hope for is that I will be able to finish strong—that I won't make any great mistakes during these last couple of years. Yes, I just want to finish strong. That's what I'm praying for."

Most everyone can identify with that. Wherever we are in life, whatever our life's journey has been, we would like to go out on a positive note. It would be embarrassing to do something disgraceful without having a chance to rectify it.

It's one thing to talk about that in connection with our careers, but this becomes especially serious when we talk about it in connection with our spiritual lives, our faith. We are eternal people, and each day of our lives has eternal significance. We go through stages; sometimes we are strong with the power of God, and other times we feel ourselves estranged from God. We have our ups and downs. We would like to be up when we cross the finish line and enter the future we have thought so much about.

The only way to finish strong is to finish with total reliance on our God and on the Lord Jesus Christ, our Savior. Jude concludes his all-too-brief words with a unique and encouraging doxology. It is God who is able to keep us from falling, and he will enable us to finish strong, not in our own strength, but in his.

The power of the Christian life—and believers do have power through the Holy Spirit—is a derivative power. Christians are powerful with the power that results from God surrounding us with his own infinite power. Jude describes this as a guarding power—the word *keep* is not nearly strong enough for what this really means. God is like a father who runs beside his little child's two-wheeler when she first learns to ride, keeping up with her, speaking a few instructions, always ready with his hand to steady the bike—God guards us from falling that way.

And God does a superior job. When a young child learns to ride, each attempt either ends in a fall, in spite of parental attention, or it ends with the child finally just stopping. Both feet suddenly go to the ground some time before the bike is fully stopped, and the child, a little bit shaken, looks at the beaming bystanders for approval. Those who trust God to put the finishing touches to their lives may know that they will not fall, and that when their earthly adventure ends, they will be presented to God himself.

To be sure, this is a fearsome prospect. Yet Jude, the half brother of Jesus, by the way, describes what will happen when we stand before him thus: we will be without fault and with great joy. There we will continue to praise him as we have been doing so feebly while here: Glory, majesty, power and authority be to our great God! We will shout it out. We will be free finally from the dreadful sin-shroud that encumbers us now each day, and we will experience an ecstasy beyond imagining.

And, Jude reminds us, it will all be because of what Jesus has done. It is all through Jesus Christ our Lord. Jesus alone is the cause of this blessed prospect, for those who believe in him. Yes, we want to finish strong in terms of our careers, our family and other social responsibilities, and in terms of our faith. We do. We don't want to do something dumb at the end. Most of all, we want to bring glory to the cause of Christ. We want much, but we are terribly weak in ourselves, infected with the sin virus that keeps cropping up.

So, forever people that we are, again in this day, we hear the call to trust in God, the true God, in God alone. We need God to surround us with his power once again. And so we turn to Jesus—all the benefits of eternal grace are ours through his finished work!

Please, O loving God, keep me from falling today. And if I should die today, please present me before your glorious presence without fault and with great joy. I pray in Jesus' name, who has taken my fault and has given me the Spirit of joy. Amen.

The Deeds That Follow

Blessed are the dead who die in the Lord. . . . For their deeds will follow them.
—Revelation 14:13

It is a marvelous thing to be a human being, created in the image of God and redeemed through the finished work of Christ Jesus. It is an inestimable, incredible wonder; no words in any language can capture the sublime mystery of it all. God brings us into existence; beginning as a thought in his mind, he ordains us to eternal life and then does all that is necessary in order to bring us finally into his glorious presence.

There is but one adjective that can catch the glory of all this: *blessed.* The blessing of all this extends to every event in a person's life, even as we begin our eternal lives already in this world. Everything we do, each thought we think, all of it is significant in the life of the child of God. And what happens in this world for each of us is the beginning of an eternal existence that will very soon become entirely perfect.

The reality of the judgment that looms so ominously at the end of the road is actually the great declaration that our lives are significant. That God takes us so seriously that he will judge us for every idle word and frivolous deed is, in reality, an enormous divine declaration that our lives are meaningful. Surely if God has arranged to judge us someday, he must take all that we do extremely seriously. We are not able to grasp the full wonder of this.

Revelation 14 contemplates the death of God's people, using the word *blessed* to describe them, and then connects that blessedness with the deeds that they do during their lives on earth. Their "works" follow them, says the venerable King James Version of the text.

Since the writer here speaks of their works in connection with their blessedness, the focus must be upon the works they have done in the power of the Spirit, the

206

good works that God gave them to do. To be sure, they have other works too that follow them, works that make them ashamed and fearful, but those works, praise God, have been covered by the blood of the crucified Lamb.

The fact that God's people will appear in glory along with their works reminds us that faith in Christ is attended by a wonderful ministry of God's Holy Spirit in the lives of his people. Ephesians 2:8-10 is both a reminder that we are saved by grace alone and an exciting description of what happens to those who are redeemed: "For it is by grace you have been saved, through faith—and this not from yourselves, it is the gift of God—not by works, so that no one can boast. For we are God's workmanship, created in Christ Jesus to do good works, which God prepared in advance for us to do."

These stirring words not only humble us with regard to our own natural potentiality—we have none whatsoever—but they also alert us to the great work of God in the lives of believers. He saves us so that we will live as Spirit-filled people who then take up the very works that God has prepared for us when he chose us to be his people.

The words from Ephesians allow us to think of each individual Christian and all believers together as God's exquisite poetry, in the sense that they are works of art. The Christian way allows us to escape from the desolate and empty life experience of those for whom life is nothing but an absurd accident, nothing but the product of mindless chance.

Our God is so breathtakingly glorious that he *personally* takes charge of every element of our lives, so that when we finally stand before God, he will view us as the product of his own handiwork. And in the case of divinity, "personally" means that each one of the holy Persons of the sacred Trinity participates in making our regeneration, our calling, our justification, our sanctification, and our glorification sure.

So those who die in the Lord carry the blessed realities of God's work in their lives. And this is true of all of them, without exception. It is as true of the humblest person whose life of faith has gone generally unnoticed, as it is true of those believers who, for whatever reason, have enjoyed a fleeting earthly prominence.

Yes, we are forever people. And what we do in this day, once more, will somehow affect our eternity.

O loving and glorious God, we marvel at the way you attend our way,
unworthy creatures that we are. But we believe that you equip and
qualify us to work the works you have prepared for us. Glorify yourself
in us again today anew. For Jesus' sake, Amen.